The Open Light

| 10/14/2013 |

AUNT BETTY—

For your pleasure, and for your quiet study.

"Rah rah rah rah rah rah rah rah rah rah rah Notre Dame."

Love,

Jack

The Open Light

Poets from Notre Dame, 1991–2008

Edited by

ORLANDO RICARDO MENES

University of Notre Dame Press

Notre Dame, Indiana

Manufactured in the United States of America

Library of Congress Cataloging-in-Publication Data

The open light : poets from Notre Dame, 1991–2008 / edited by Orlando
Ricardo Menes.
        p.   cm.
    Includes bibliographical references.
    ISBN-13: 978-0-268-03521-1 (pbk. : alk. paper)
    ISBN-10: 0-268-03521-0 (pbk. : alk. paper)
    1. American poetry—Indiana—Notre Dame.   2. University of Notre Dame.
I. Menes, Orlando Ricardo.
    PS572.N68O74   2011
    811'.6080977289—dc20
                        2010049967

 This book was printed on recycled paper.

for my colleagues

John Matthias and Sonia Gernes

Contents

Preface

Twenty years after the publication in 1991 of Professor James Walton's *The Space Between: Poets from Notre Dame, 1950–1990*, this follow-up anthology aims to celebrate again poetry's vital presence at the University of Notre Dame. It uses the same criteria for inclusion: that the poet was associated with the university during the years indicated, and has published at least one full-length collection (not necessarily during those years). In the case of several poets, there were multiple books to consider, containing poems written over decades-long careers, which meant that I had to winnow my choices to a handful or so and thereby exclude some worthy poems. I finally settled on those poems that in my judgment adroitly exemplify the poet's specific aesthetic, while at the same time appealing to a general audience curious about Notre Dame's poetic culture. The craft of writing, in particular that of verse, has long held a position of esteem at Notre Dame, all the way back to the 1860s, when student poems, most often imitating classical models and the prevailing poetics of the Victorian era, would appear regularly in the weekly *Scholastic* magazine. There were also bound volumes of prize-winning poems every year from 1917 to 1923, culminating in 1927 with *The Notre Dame Anthology*, edited by Professor Charles Phillips.

Looking at the table of contents in Walton's *The Space Between*, one notices such luminaries as John Frederick Nims, John Logan, Anthony Kerrigan, and Michael Ryan, among others, as well as the much admired and beloved Professor Ernest Sandeen, who sadly passed away in 1997, and the now retired John Matthias and Sonia Gernes. During their tenure at Notre Dame, Matthias and Gernes made pivotal contributions to culture, both on campus and beyond it. One need only read these poets' statements in the back of this anthology to realize how many students they influenced and supported. Those who come readily to mind, and who are represented in the current anthology, include Robert Archambeau and Joe Doerr, who not only received their Master of Fine Arts degrees at Notre Dame but also wrote Ph.D. dissertations directed by Matthias. As poets, in fact, their fondness for the modernist sequence is an obvious sign of Matthias's tutelage. Others included here, such as Mary Hawley, praise Gernes, whose influence can be seen in the narrative lyric and in what might be called a poetics of empathy, which she has long championed. Sandeen also had a notable impact on the writing careers of Anthony Walton and John Phillip Santos while they were still undergraduates.

Of course, much has changed since the publication of Walton's anthology in 1991. Creative writing has undoubtedly grown more essential to the intellectual identity and artistic ambitions of Notre Dame, as evidenced by the founding in 1991 of our flourishing Creative Writing Program, which has garnered considerable praise from the literary establishment. This is in large part because of the accomplishments of our M.F.A. graduates, who have published novels and poetry collections with both commercial publishers and independent presses. Other achievements include several AWP Intro Awards and even the prestigious APR/Honickman First Book Prize, won by Kevin Ducey in 2004 for his collection *Rhinoceros* (judged by Yusef Komunyakaa). Ducey is indeed a poet of irresistible panache and wit, so I am delighted that I was able to include five of his poems. As a program, we are also proud of the establishment of *The Notre Dame Review*, whose poems and short stories have subsequently appeared in the *Best American Series*, and the Ernest Sandeen Poetry Prize (eight collections strong as of 2011). Thanks to generous grants from Notre Dame's Institute for Scholarship in the Liberal Arts, we have sponsored such exciting conferences as "The Long Reach of African-American Poetics" in 2006, "& Now: A Festival of Writing as a Contemporary Art" in 2004, and the "Latino Poets Conference" in 2002. Our reading series has brought to campus numerous authors, both from the United States and abroad, including the Nobel Prize nominee Bei Dao, who also taught at Notre Dame as a visiting professor between 2005 and 2007. Four of his poems grace these pages.

Our Creative Writing faculty has changed considerably over the years. I joined the program in 2000 as an assistant professor, while still in my first year of teaching at the University of Dayton. Later on, Cornelius Eady and Joyelle McSweeney would replace John Matthias and Sonia Gernes. Steve Tomasula also joined William O'Rourke and Valerie Sayers as the third fiction writer in the program.

The Open Light, a title I took from Professor Eady's poem "Why Was I Born? A Duet between John Coltrane and Kenny Burrell," is a fortuitous metaphor for the explosion of diversity that has taken place since the publication of Walton's The Space Between. Women constitute more than one-third of the poets in this second volume; regrettably, the proportions are still not close to parity. Walton himself lamented the dearth of women's voices, especially in light of Notre Dame's long exclusion of women as undergraduates, which did not formally end until 1972, when the first female undergraduates were enrolled. The situation of women poets has dramatically changed since then. For example, Jacque Vaught Brogan, among the first three women tenured in our English Department, and a prolific scholar of modern American literature, has had her first poetry collection, entitled Damage, published by the University of Notre Dame Press. Graduates such as Jenny Boully (M.F.A. 2002) and Kimberly Blaeser (Ph.D. 1990) have forged successful careers as both writers and as academics. Boully's poems and lyric essays have appeared in many journals and in collections published by Sarabande and The Essay Press. Blaeser is an English professor at the University of Wisconsin-Milwaukee, teaching creative writing and Native American Literature. She is the author of a critical study of Gerald Vizenor as well as three poetry collections. Beth Ann Fennelly is a celebrated young poet, whose work has appeared in the Best American Poetry series, and who currently teaches in the Creative Writing Program at the University of Mississippi. As her own statement explains, it was during her undergraduate years at Notre Dame that she came to realize her poetic vocation. These women's accomplishments are a strong predictor that many more will go on to find professional success, whether in the publication of their work, in academia, or in the editorial field.

Another significant element of The Open Light is the number of ethnic groups represented—African Americans, Latinos, Asian

Americans, Native Americans—at times sharing a common Catholic heritage, but not always. Our strength, perhaps, lies in the encompassing definition of the word "catholic" as a synonym for the universal, and thus we find a sizeable contingent of international poets. I wish to emphasize, however, that this plethora of voices proves even more enticing if we consider the poems themselves, and how they differ and yet somehow converge, whether in thematic concerns, in style, or in form. It is a treat to read the snazzy, blues-infused poetry of Cornelius Eady, the co-founder of Cave Canem (a non-profit organization fostering contemporary African American poetry) and the author of numerous poetry collections, alongside the work of Anthony Walton, author of the well-received memoir *Mississippi: An American Journey* and co-editor with Michael Harper of *The Vintage Book of African American Poetry*. This anthology also displays convergences among ethnicities and geographies. Francisco Aragón (M.F.A. 2003), born in San Francisco to Nicaraguan parents and a resident of Spain for nearly a decade, shares with Tom O'Grady (Ph.D. 1984), a native of Canada's eastern coast, a preoccupation with displacement and uprootedness in this time of globalization. The author of one poetry collection, O'Grady is Professor of English, Director of Irish Studies, and a member of the Creative Writing faculty at the University of Massachusetts in Boston. Aragón worked as an English teacher in Madrid and Barcelona, while at the same time honing the craft of translation, which explains the bilingual format of *Puerta del Sol*, his first full-length collection. Since receiving his M.F.A., Aragón has worked at Notre Dame's Institute for Latino Studies, where he now directs the unit Letras Latinas, which he himself created and which houses, among other things, the bi-annual Andrés Montoya Poetry Prize, our nation's sole prize dedicated to publishing a Latino/a poet's first book. John Phillip Santos, a Mexican American and author of the acclaimed memoir *Places Left Unfinished at the Time of Creation*, has written poems rich in the cross-cultural imagination and immersed in particular confluences of history and culture. Santos's intellectually restless voice and passion for experimentation are qualities that he shares with the Canadian-born Archambeau, the English John Wilkinson, and the Americans Joe Doerr, Stacy Cartledge, Michael Smith, and Michael Coffey. Thomas O'Grady's formalist poetics (see his brilliant sestina

"Lament for My Family, Lost at Sea") also finds an affinity with the sonnets and couplets of the Canadian-born Henry Weinfield, a professor in Notre Dame's Program for Liberal Studies. Poets whose roots lie (at least partially) in Asia include Jenny Boully and Karni Pal Bhati. Boully was born in Thailand to a Thai mother and an American father and raised in Texas, and much of her poetry is concerned with this dual heritage. Bhati, who earned both an M.F.A. and a Ph.D. from Notre Dame, writes about his Indian birthplace and upbringing in vivid detail. Kimberly Blaeser, a Native American, is one more vital voice in this rich panoply of American ethnic identity, one that speaks to the often overlooked (and very current) estrangement between the more assimilated Native Americans and their tribal communities.

I hope that you will agree that the poems in *The Open Light* demonstrate a remarkable range of talent and accomplishment and portend an even more exciting future for poetry at Notre Dame.

Acknowledgments

Francisco Aragón. "Madrid in July," "February Snow," Winter Sun," and "Tricycles" from *Puerta del Sol* (Bilingual Press/Editorial Bilingüe). Grateful acknowledgement is given to Bilingual Press/Editorial Bilingüe Press for permission to reprint these poems.

Robert Archambeau. "Two Short Films," "Turkish Engraving," "Misremembering Szymborska," and "Imitations and Collage: from the Poems of Blas de Otero" from *Home and Variations* (Salt). Copyright © 2004 by Robert Archambeau. Reprinted by permission of the author.

Bei Dao. "February," "Showing Up," "Old Places," and "Borders" from *Landscape Over Zero* (New Directions). Copyright © 1995, 1996 by Zhao Zhenkai (Bei Dao). Translation copyright © 1995, 1996 by David Hinton with Yanbing Chen. Reprinted by permission of New Directions Publishing Corp.

Karni Pal Bhati. "Books," "Theology," "A Hike on Bikes," and "Dwellings" from *On Another Ground* (Ninety-Six Press). Copyright © 2006 by Karni Pal Bhati. Reprinted by permission of the author.

Kimberly M. Blaeser. "Ice Tricksters and Shadow Stories" and "On the Way to the Chicago Pow-Wow" from *Trailing You* (Greenfield Review Press). Copyright © 1994 by Kimberly M. Blaeser. Reprinted by permission of the author. "Absentee Indians" and "March 1998: Seeking Solace" from *Absentee Indians and Other Poems* (Michigan State University Press). Copyright © 2002 by Kimberly Blaeser. Reprinted by permission of the author.

Jenny Boully. Footnotes 58, 59, 60, 61, 68, 69, 136, 137, 138, and 139 from *The Body* (Slope Editions). Copyright © 2002 by Jenny Boully. Reprinted by permission of the author.

Jacque Vaught Brogan. "Window," "Stable," and sections ii, viii, ix, and xiv from "Notes from the Body" from *Damage* (University of Notre Dame Press). Copyright © 2003 by Jacque Vaught Brogan. Reprinted by permission of the author.

Stacy Cartledge. "inertia," "divine comedy," "evanescent," and "codex (a discourse)" from *Within the Space Between*. Reprinted by permission of the author and Spuyten Duyvil.

Michael Coffey. "Lawrentian" and "A Fact of Language" from *Elemenopy* (Sun & Moon Press). Copyright © 1996 by Michael Coffey. Reprinted by permission of the author. "Melville on the Beach" and "Dad's Shoes" from *87 North* (Coffee House Press). Copyright © 1999 by Michael Coffey. Reprinted by permission of the author. "Ideas of Order" from *87 CMYK* (O Books). Copyright © 2005 by Michael Coffey. Reprinted by permission of the author.

Seamus Deane. "Smoke Signals in Oregon" from *Gradual Wars* (Irish University Press). Copyright © 1972 by Seamus Deane. Reprinted by permission of the author. "Migration" and "Shelter" from *Rumours* (Humanities Press). Copyright © 1977 by Seamus Deane. Reprinted by permission of the author. "History Lessons" from *History Lessons* (Gallery Books). Copyright © 1983 by Seamus Deane. Reprinted by permission of the author.

Joe Francis Doerr. "January Thaw," "Star-crossed," "Sestina for the Birds," and "A Piece of September" from *Order of the Ordinary* (Salt). Copyright © 2003 by Joe Francis Doerr. Reprinted by permission of the author.

Kevin Ducey. "Dien Bien Phu," "Homo Habilis: The Tool Maker," "Heretic," "Lamentations," and "Wim Wenders Versus the Wolf Man" from *Rhinoceros* (The APR/Honickman First Book Prize, The Ameri-

by Joyelle McSweeney. Reprinted by permission of the author. "What I Eat Is a Prayer" and "The Born Fetus" from *The Commandrine and Other Poems* (Fence Books). Copyright © 2006 by Joyelle McSweeney. Reprinted by permission of the author.

Orlando Ricardo Menes. "Fish Heads" from *Rumba atop the Stones* (Peepal Tree Press). Copyright © 2001 by Orlando Ricardo Menes. Reprinted by permission of the author. "Hair" and "Miami, South Kendall, 1969" from *Furia* (Milkweed Editions). Copyright © 2005 by Orlando Ricardo Menes. Reprinted by permission of the author. "Ars Poetica" and "*Zafra*" used by permission of the author.

Thomas O'Grady. "Exile," "Lament for My Family, Lost at Sea," "War Stories," "Thanksgiving," and "Epithalamia" from *What Really Matters* (McGill-Queen's University Press). Copyright © 2000 by Thomas O'Grady. Reprinted by permission of the author.

John Phillip Santos. "Piedras Negras," "The Fredericksburg Screen," "Epistle on History," and "La Diosa de Maguey" from *Songs Older Than Any Known Singer: Selected and New Poems, 1974–2006* (Wings Press). Copyright © 2007 by John Phillip Santos. Reprinted by permission of the author.

Michael Smith. "Anagrammatic Ode to Emily Dickinson" and "Small Industry" from *The Possibility of Language: Seven New Poets*, ed. Jeffrey Roessner (Samizdat Editions). Copyright © 2001 by Samizdat Editions. Reprinted by permission of Samizdat Editions.

Anthony Walton. "Third Shift," "Elegy for Joan (1955–1986)," and "Insomnia" from *Cricket Weather* (Blackberry Books). Copyright © 1995 by Anthony Walton. Reprinted by permission of the author. "McDonald's, Scottsboro, April, 1997" and "Gwendolyn Brooks" from *Rainbow Darkness: An Anthology of African American Poetry*, ed. Keith Tuma (Miami University Press). Copyright © 2005 by Miami University Press. Reprinted by permission of the author.

Henry Weinfield. Sonnets two, three, six, and seven from *Sonnets Elegiac and Satirical*, "An Essay on Violence," and "Song for the In-Itself and For-Itself" all from *The Sorrows of Eros and Other Poems* (University of Notre Dame Press). Copyright © 1999 by Henry Weinfield. Reprinted by permission of the author.

John Wilkinson. "Facing Port Talbot" from *Effigies Against the Light* (Salt). Copyright © 2001 by John Wilkinson. Reprinted by permission of the author. "London Fields From Afar" and "Better the Fence" from *Contrivances* (Salt). Copyright © 2003 by John Wilkinson. Reprinted by permission of the author. "Marram Grass" from *Lake Shore Drive* (Salt). Copyright © 2006 by John Wilkinson. Reprinted by permission of the author.

FRANCISCO ARAGÓN

Madrid in July

The whirling breath
of dryers left open;
the blood that thrives

whenever I glimpse
the hair on his wrist—
picturing those hands

and how they prepare
salmon: removing each bone,
the body peeled and smoked

so clients can dine
in style, he says;
he and I folding,

stacking well into the afternoon
tablecloths and napkins
and once, a rare

summer sky: blue
and silver sheet approaching
electric with rain

—those sudden drops
cool as we step
from the fragrant

laundry air,
refreshed and alert
the four blocks home.

February Snow

The tint of the sky between sunset and night.

And wandering with you and your nephew
in that maze, half-lost—*Madrid
of the Austrias*—looking for Plaza of the Green

Cross where, days before you arrived,
an Opel with false plates was parked, its wheels
straddling the curb, and so the van

heading for the barracks that morning
had to slow to squeeze
past . . . Back at the hotel your mom

is holding up her gift—Amethyst, she says
admiring how light
when passing through a prism

bends. At his window that morning before we began
my student said, ¡Qué bonito!, watching it drift
and descend, settling on roofs and cars.

And I think of you and your wife
and daughter; getting to see Madrid
in white, your visit winding down, and how

I had wanted that lesson to end
to get to the park—Retiro, they say, is the city's
one lung, and the way the feel and sound of steps

cease
when grass is completely covered
as if walking on a cloud. The year before

on a visit from the coast, a friend
sitting at a window
watched the flakes flutter

and fall, dissolving before reaching
the ground—aguanieve, he said
while from a town near Seville

B-52s were lifting off . . .
I was in a trance that week
though like most things the war

in the Gulf was soon another
backdrop, like the string of car bombs
the following year. And yet that morning

as soon as I heard, something led me
not to the park but down
to City Hall, workers in the street

evacuated, sipping coffee, though I never reached
the site—of course it was cordoned
off, the spray of glass, the heap

of twisted metal, and so later learned their names
their lives. Of the five
there was one: a postal clerk who

as a boy, would plunge his hands
into the white, the cold
a sweet jolt

whenever he got to touch
the stuff, scooping
it tightly into a ball

like the ones he would dodge and throw
years later
at his wife-to-be: those weekends,

those places—away from city air—
a release . . . Miraflores, Siete
Picos, Rascafría . . . *It's in*

his blood, she would come to say
chatting with a neighbor
about his thing for snow—the way it falls

softly, blanketing roofs
and groves, villages
nestled in the Sierra's

hills: it is February
and she is picturing him
and the boy, up there now

playing, horsing around

Winter Sun

That my student the banker phoned
to cancel his 3 o'clock
is what triggered it, sparing

me the subway car—half my days
spent underground (as teaching on site
demands)—allowing instead

a walk in the winter sun, this unhurried
errand—picking up a new
pair of glasses—producing in me

a mood I'm trying to name, the air
—after last night's storm—
crisp enough to taste, sprinkled

with sputtering vespas and horns,
the newly scrubbed neoclassic
façades along Alcalá

and faces, faces glanced
or gazed at, waiting for the light
to change, as it did ten years

ago when I was first a student
in Spain: the last class of the week
finished and so I'd stroll

to the port—not sidewalks along the street
but one wide walk, traffic streaming up
and down, both sides of it: La Rambla—

past merchant pavilions on my right
and left: newsagents, florists, pet
sellers and their chirping cages

the year I lived on the Mediterranean
meeting, my second week there,
Sandra & Bob—we sold

our cottage in Bournemouth
so we could navigate, live
docked in a port city a stretch

and sail to the next, she said, lathering
up a little dog, Sandra
& Bob, those walks to the harbor, sipping

tea into the early evening on their boat, home
away from home until they headed
back to England that spring, the adventure

altered, failed, the shadow of their absence
for weeks after they left
difficult to name, as it's hard to name

this, the opposite: something, perhaps,
approaching exhilaration,
subdued joy—those Fridays in college

I didn't cross the bay to the City,
and would meet her
—who'd taken BART

for me—at Mario's on Telegraph
and Haste: tamales, beans, and rice
on a huge plate . . . It's been a year

and a day. A year and a day since I was sailing
west across the states,
the 767 hugging the earth,

and she below, her breathing
labored, slowly drifting away

Tricycles

~ to my mother (1932–1997)

Metal-gray, sturdy—
those heavy-duty ones we rode
on Fridays: being led
out of a bright church
basement and through swinging
glass doors into that dim
seemingly round room—hardwood
floor we circled counter
clockwise pedaling and
pedaling with exuberant deter-
mination, as if to play
were a serious matter, which
it was: me and a friend climbing
off, leaving them riderless,

sneaking up spiral stairs, exploring
the pews, organ chamber, statue
of what looked like—I never told you—
a lipsticked Virgin, the chemical
smell of synthetic carpet

—burned, torn down two terms
after we "graduated": the empty lot
we'd pass heading for Cala
Foods (you'd let me push
the cart) for years wild with weeds
till it became the space
it is today, *The Palm Broker*
selling trees on Guerrero Street
                    —it's now
I know
the shield you were those frugal years

And the long-haired man
who sat in the sandbox
with us on warm days—once,
after it fell from my hands, I ate
a crunchy noisy sandwich;
I thought he was a Beatle, driving
you mad: *Revolution* screeching
over and over on Maria's
turntable at home

And the black and white
photograph snapped of me
I glimpsed in a manila envelope

the other day—the moving
picture in my head
sharpening into focus
                 of you
in that basement
crouching at a low table:
those geometric shapes
like stained glass only plastic
the click and snap of attaching
them to each other—helping me
for ten, fifteen minutes
before whispering
in my ear, disappearing behind

the door I rise toward when I grow
tired of waiting. What is it
exactly, I'm feeling
when I see you're gone, that brings
wetness to my cheeks, wetness
absent decades later before
your casket? What was it
I began to lose
that first day? How well
you knew me then, knowing
that tricking me
                 was how
that first morning
you'd get me to stay

ROBERT ARCHAMBEAU

Two Short Films

on the translation of the European imagination to America

. . . what we feel of sorrow and despair
From ruin and from change, and all the grief
The passing shews of being leave behind,
Appeared an idle dream . . . .
                    Wordsworth, *The Prelude*

Up to now literature has exalted a pensive immobility, ecstasy,
and sleep. We intend to exalt aggressive action, a feverish insomnia . . .
                    Marinneti, *Futurist Manifesto*

1. Wordsworth at the Cuyahoga's Mouth, 1796–1996

In newsreel stock, in jumpy monochrome
You mount the windy bluff, glance back and turn
To face the valley. Far below, white water foams

Birds cry, and black waves peel from slabs of rock,
Back down to the great lake's boom and suck.
You stand, a silhouette, black coat and stick.

The film moves quickly now—clouds fly and light's
A flickered blur of days and nights. You wait,
The still point of a world that's turned to haste.

You wait, and plowed lines break the dark earth's crust—
The valley peopled now—and frontier huts
Crop up each harvest time. A rail line thrusts

On past that limestone ridge, with quick faint wraiths
That, caught in a frame that stutters through the gate,
Are horses, wagons, wide-backed men. You wait,

Brick chimneys frame the screen and black smoke swells,
A furnace-city churns its molten steel—
And one quick night's a flash: city plays hell.

And you, above this growth and flux and ruin,
Does your sleepwalker-muse fetch Whitman songs
Great port, great ore-port, great handler of iron—

Or bring *an image of tranquility*
So calm and still, a green dream's tapestry
Of soft grass overgrowing history?

I can't expect an answer: You stand, there,
And breathe the flickered light of setting suns, the living air.

2. Marinetti at Union Station, Chicago

Arrived, the locomotive paws the tracks,
deep-chested, bellowing

(we gather, from this silent reel);
its steam-plumes jet in cavern air

beneath the city. And, arrived—
in the city of railyards,

apparatus, of stokers groping blackened
through the mill-fire's angry blast,

the city of shipping, chemical manufacture,
stockyards blazed with electric moons—you,

mounting the platform, gestures broad,
erratic, oratorical.

Saying (we barely see, white letters
over faded stock) *Hold no ideal mistress high,*

her form divine rising to touch clouds;
saying *All must be swept aside,*

to express our whirling life of steel, of pride,
of fever and exalted speed;

saying, in that rush of sailors, workmen,
quick-eyed thieves, *death to Ciceroni, antiquarians* . . .

Mechanic-limbed and darting, the crowd
won't pause to hear you, and I

wonder, do you dream of Venice,
soft, past-loving, shocked

in all her statuary, when you declared
The first dawn is now, an explosive breath?

You, erratic, oratorical, the last frame
fading on your words, *our bodies die for speed*

for movement and for darting light.

Turkish Engraving

Were they wrong about decline, those men
Who etched in copper urbane scenes? These plates
Of coffeehouses, streets, the marketplace,
Interstices of life, should these condemn
Their makers, who saw days fill up with talk
And trade, backgammon, dark flirtatious eyes,
Hands nimbly plucking strings to song—all while
They knew the armies fled the field, exports dropped,
And rats' feet crept on dozing tramps down by the quays?
Perhaps they felt the measure of decay
Too large to matter much. Each, in his way
Could capture pleasures, living privately.
Good coffee steams in our cafés and we, like them,
Hide hunger for solutions from our friends.

Misremembering Szymborska

I read your poem in a magazine, the one about how
after every war, someone

has to tidy up, about how,
as years trudge on with shovel and with trowel,

bridges are rebuilt, windows glazed, doors set back
into their jambs, until someone,

propped broom in an arm's neat crook, a hand-back wiping
at his brow, tells how it was to a nodding neighbor, until

the task-bound crowd of a rebuilt city finds such talk
a little boring,

until those who were there
are gone, and those who knew them, until, at last,

someone lies in the grass, over all the old and rusted arguments,
"a corn stalk in his teeth,

gawking at clouds." I read it, there, but
remembered it differently. Somehow

in the tired and task-bound wearied mind those final,
placid, resting limbs

became a body *in* the earth, not on it,
a corn stalk growing from that place in which it lay.

I see your poem now, again, "The End and the Beginning,"
and know I've carried my mistake for months.

That soldier I remembered—that's what he must have been,
that body under the earth—he would have dreamed

of days spent gawking, on a hillside, at the clouds.
Perhaps he fought for just such days, that he should have them, perhaps

that dream is where he lingers even now.
Perhaps he can lie beneath your dreamer, a tightness, there,

each in his way the other's end. Perhaps, too,
we could say my poem lies in the grass of your poem's dreaming,

forgetful, pulls at corn stalks, gawks at sky.

Imitations and Collage:
from the Poems of Blas de Otero

1. From Each According to What He Knows
a version of Otero's "Que Cada Uno Aporte Lo Que Sepa"

It's true, you know: you *can* love a person,
a little toad—don't step on it—

and also a continent like Europe,
always split or wounded or crying horribly.

Some words disturb us, you and me,
"treaty," "theater of operations,"

"end of major fighting," "nothing serious,"
and others too.

But people, they believe all that,
hang bunting, run flags out the windows,

as if it were true,
as if such a thing . . .

It happens—I've seen them myself,
all Easter hats and roses.

In '39 they called the poor men out to Mass,
pulled fuses from a few bombs,

and set off fireworks along the water:
at it again.

After, I heard voices in the next room,
a woman screaming, mad and awful.

We knew,
we knew more than enough.

2. Words Gathered for Antonio Machado
a version of Otero's "Palabras Reunidas Para Antonio Machado"

>   *a solitary heart*
>   *is no heart*
>   —A.M.

If I dared
to speak, to call for you . . .
but I am, alone,
no one.

So.
I clench my fists and look to your root-place,
I listen to slow yesterday,
her ballads, all the people's songs—
rough Manrique, exact Fray Luis,
the quick-whip words of old Quevedo—
and quick, too,
I touch the earth that has lost you,
and the sea that holds a ship that must find home.

And now,
now the plow has turned in salted soil,
now I'll say *a few true words*,
those with which I first sought a voice:

>   *Elm sonorous with wind,*
>   *tall poplar, sluggish oak and olive,*
>   *trees of a dry land, and of sorrow—*
>   *come to clear water, to freedom, to peace*

Sevilla cries. Soria, for once,
grows quiet. Baeza
lifts her sickles to the air, her olive trees
slow-moving to the wind's soft sorrow, which she reaps.
The sea itself falls fast on France to claim you—
it wants,
we want,
to have you here,
            to share you out
like bread.

3. The Cloister of Shadows
a version of Otero's "El Claustro de las Sombras"

> *. . . to the antique order of the dead*
> —Francis Thompson

Just now I have thirty-three years piled on my study table
and a few months left over in the silver ashtray.
I've put this question to my sisters: do you know this man
between my left and right shoulders? He goes where I go,
and turns his face if I turn mine . . .

I grow cold, and don't know what to wear
beneath this cloaking death, don't know what plot of earth is mine,
what night I should prepare,
what green and silent ocean waits . . .

Sometimes I'd be a brother of the ancient order of the dead
and serve in silence; meditate in a corner of the dead,

in the cloister of shadows, there,
where dreams rise guileless in the smoky light.

4. Collage: The Public Life

If you reap a soft, slow moving sorrow,
If you gather years in a silver ashtray,

If you wait, a green and silent ocean,
If you serve the antique order of yourself,

If, at your study table,
you know, you know too much—

can you love a person, or a continent?
Can you turn and share yourself like bread?

BEI DAO

February

night approaching perfection
I float amid languages
the brasses in death's music
full of ice

who's up over the crack in day
singing, water turns bitter
bled flames pale
leaping like leopards toward stars
to dream
you need a form

in the cold morning
an awakened bird
comes closer to truth
as I and my poems
sink together

february in the book:
certain movements and shadows

Showing Up

in childhoods of broken grammar blooming
we don't say much
roam life
watch oceans beyond fences
seasons by which we traveled
plunge in

music perfectly cold and cruel
marriage neatly strewn
someone sick of this world
walks toward a definite address
like smoke vanishing

endless waves of sorrow
hurry children out of bed
sunlight gathers & scatters
we don't say much

Old Places

death's always on the other side
watching the painting

at the window just now
I saw a sunset from my youth
visiting old places again
I'm anxious to tell the truth
but before the skies go dark
what more can be said

drinking a cup of words
only makes you thirstier
I join riverwater to quote the earth
and listen in empty mountains
to the flute player's sobbing heart

angels collecting taxes
return from the painting's other side
from those gilded skulls
taking inventory clear into sunset

Borders

storms turn toward the north's future
sick people's roots howl underground
a sun propeller
chases bees until they're rays of light
messengers in chains
sow seed in those ears long for the wind

remembered rivers
never end
stolen sound
becomes borders

borders allow no hope
a book
swallows a wing
and still in the hard ice of language
brothers redeem their crimes
you struggle on for this

KARNI PAL BHATI

Books

i

In my mother's house were holy books
large and bound, wrapped in red cloth
stacked on ledges past the reach of little
unwashed hands quick to spot picture-pages
to gape unhurried at mace-wielding Hanuman
leaping out of a female ogre's mouth
or vulture-winged Jatayu facing
the big-bicepped sword-flashing Ravan.

But why was it always RamBachanji, the venerable Brahmin—
who filled the afternoons reading out of
those tomes while relatives and visitors,
men and women, nodded in unison, fanning themselves
or breaking into commentaries just to stay awake—
when we could have done just as well?

ii

In my father's house were almost no books
or so we thought, until he found the time in retirement
to unbox his collection and out came regimental histories
with frontispieces of Colonels of the Regiment of Grenadiers,
British and Indian (past and present), obscure old novels,
pamphlets on bandobust for ceremonial occasions,
Urdu primers and textbooks on infantry combat
in romanized Hindustani.
                              I don't know how much he
                              cared for

them, but they sit snugly amid commentaries on the *Gita*,
the *Upanishads*, and life-time subscriptions to journals
from obscure *ashrams* ministering to needs beyond
careers—these he annotated with heavily pencilled margins
proclaiming: Very Important for Boys!

Theology

My God didn't die,
young or old;
I simply left him sitting
stone-faced under the dog-desecrated
shade of a thorny shrub
with ripe red berries.

I went round him twice
in clockwise circles—
as I do today, ceaselessly in
every direction, despite this distance—
before boarding a bus
on the journey to a godless cosmopolis.

But He was certainly there
when at dusk I lent my faint voice
to a sonorous choir
of devout men of the family,
as I watched their rapt faces
in the glow of the *ghee*-fed flames.

The praying was endless,
while we children waited for the
palm-bestowed coconut-'n'-jaggery,
washed down with the obligatory
ash-flavored water.
This done, we dragged our feet

—avoiding thorns—a few tentative
yards, to where our shoes lay.
Noisily huddling close
and holding hands to scare away fears,
our gang walked back
to the house in the dark.

A Hike on Bikes

Doubled down on handles, our scarves flying back
we labored up climbs and raced down slopes,
pedaling on through wind and traffic.
The road lay like a huge black stripe on the
undulating back of some time-torn beast.
The jamuns and tamarinds tempting us,
the big banyan shades inviting: we managed, for
the most part, to deny ourselves till we reached
that lake on the other side of Yehanapattahalli,
waving on our way to its staring folk and
their little children cheering us.
                              And later in the shade
of a pine-grove near the lake we killed the
fish we'd caught, knocking their heads against
stones, and cooked them over a fire of twigs.

Dwellings

~ for JM

1

> *A lytle house wel fylled A lytle grounde wel*
> *tylled And a little wife wel willed is best.*

Deep in the impenetrable palimpsest of utterance,
a hus, hows, hous, huus, houus, huse, huis,
howise, houss, howse, owse, hws.
      "The ultimate etymology is uncertain:
      it has been with some probability referred
      to the verbal root *hud-*, *hûd-* of hydan to HIDE,
               Aryan *keudh-*, . . .
      but other suggestions have also been offered."
         Where or by whom, is unsaid.

A house, a building for human habitation.
The Sanskrit *griha*: singular, masculine.
    1. house, dwelling; home.
    2. building or room assigned to a special purpose.
Ghar: the same in Urdu-Hindi, Rajasthani, Gujarati,
                  Marathi, Nepali, etc.
Also a receptacle of any kind,
             as in house of water.
And further down the path,
         a twelfth part of the very heavens.

A house-farmer's populous household
with its house-gods, house-flies, house-boy,
house-mice, house-sparrows, house-spiders,
house-cat, house-dog and those ones housed in
         the oxe hous near the hey howse,

besides other visitors and residents
        that come hopping and crawling out
with the lighting of the evening lamp
        in the soot-blackened niche under the eaves
            to be chased by kittens across the courtyard,
not to forget the house-wife in house-clothes
with her house-work beginning
        at dawn and ending well after dark.

        But who dwells in the house unseen,
        a tenant without a lease?

2

Ducking and dodging through
eight chambers and nine doorways
have I roamed
O save me mother
for they come to take me away . . . she sang
in words that puzzle me across the miles
and these lengthening decades.

Sobbing under the bridal veil
she crossed that natal threshold
(*Right foot first. Always!* they said
trying to court the right omens),
borne away in a caparisoned cart at fifteen
to a house full of strangers
the girl grew to call family.

No longer an inmate who
crossed this doorway to give alms,
rushed in with news of goings-on elsewhere,
or called out to playmates across it—
she returned a guest from a desert place
a day's ride away.

Days and weeks grew shorter on those visits
until on the appointed day
her heart sank when girlfriends rushed in
with news of her in-laws, spotted from terraces,
arriving to take her back
to that distant house now called hers.

Decades later, the house she was born in
crouches in the quiet dark of her mind,
claimed by trees and bushes
in whose shadows owls, peacocks, dogs and snakes
loll the afternoons away hiding from one another
but staying on to hear the still echoing

jubilant cries of all her seven siblings
who did not live to play marbles and tops,
or scamper through the breezy courtyard
as monsoon clouds gathered to stir hopes
of change in the dry hot months.
The kitchen, once bounteous, its granaries

now gaping open-mouthed at the sky
its thatched roof now caved in,
its floor cracked, rubbled, heaped with sand;
that adjoining room with high ledges—
with those books that brought piety
to some, and escape to others—

is now house to geckos, honey-bees and wasps,
flitting in and out unobstructed
by the door so dexterously prized loose
with its frame by cousins who helped themselves
to whatever they found handy.
Stones on the steps leading up to the threshold

have tumbled out of place,
the house-deities on the raised platform—
their last offerings picked clean
by birds and black ants—
sit in miffed silence neither guarding
nor welcoming memories that swirl through the house.

3

Some *Grahyasutras*

A brahmin should select the site for
building his house on white ground,
a *ksatriya* on red, a *vaisya* on black.
                    And what about the sudras, O great sages?

The ground should be even,
covered with grass, not saline,
not dry.
            Water should flow off there to the northwest.
                        If there were water.

Plants with milky juice or with thorns or also
acid plants should not be there.

Soil on which darbha grass grows brings
spiritual preeminence; big sorts of grass,
strength; tender grass, cattle . . .

Now follows the putting up of the water-barrel.
            To the north-east he the householder digs a pit
            like the pit for the sacrificial post, strews into it kusa
grass, unhusked grains, fruits of the soap-tree,
and other auspicious things; and therein he

establishes
    the water-barrel with the words,
        "Thou art the sea."

    The ceremony of ploughing,

accomplished after the plough has been yoked,
requires the cooking of a mess of sacrificial
food (*sthalipaka*),
    sacrificing to Indra,

        the Maruts,
Parjanya (Rain),   Asani (Lightning),
Bhaga (Good Fortune),   Sita (furrow) etc.

    These deities receive
        similar
offerings at the furrow sacrifice,
   the threshing-floor sacrifice,
      the sowing and
the reaping of the crop and
      at the putting
  of the crop into the barn.

At molehills
    the king of moles
       should not be forgotten.

4

There are no closets in this house, nor any furniture to speak of,
you can be sure. A rope stretched across the walls serves to hang the
few clothes this family, now reduced to four, needs. Light from the
courtyard

reaches into the room's dark showing patches of rust on
the sloping corrugated-tin roof, brightening the manila shirt of the
ten-year-old boy leaning against the dull blue of the door-flap,
revealing parts of the

bare cement-grey floor where Umli, now single mother with
a three-year old daughter in her lap, squats between the two halves
of the wooden door with frame marked in auspicious red and yellow.
Eyes swollen with

days of weeping over her husband's desperate decision, left
arm stretched towards her eight-year-old girl bare-footed in flowery
frock of synthetic cloth and gilt-coated red bangles. In her ear-
length hair and round cheeks

the girl stares back with a hard curiosity while her brother
looks on with shy uncertainty, still unaccustomed to being the
object of strangers' sympathy. "Umli's husband, a farmer in hi-tech
Andhra's

Mahboobnagar district," reads the caption, "sowed paddy
to harvest death. As the crop withered away on the dry fields singed
by a merciless sun, Betavati Ratan chose to end his life leaving his
widow behind with three children to feed and a few mortgage papers
to reclaim."

5

Thirst digs deep wells of open entrails
drying in the sand-carrying wind
slaking itself at the pores on the sun-baked
        skins of toiling bodies.

Hunger sinks its talons on the flanks of
unborn calves tearing and tugging
at exposed genitals of the masses of
putrefying tissue and bone
                    that once had a form and name.

Stone and sand and bark of tree
and pegs for cows to be milked at
and empty baskets they fed in
                    all blanched.

Dry troughs fill up with sand at the
deserted village well where crows
perch on the rope-less pulley
their cries echoing
            upward into the cloudless sky.

A family of famine-stricken villagers
sits under a thin-stemmed acacia
to rest   before returning
to endless hammering and breaking
rocks to size for use in distant cement
factories or to lay a new road in a village
yet un-linked
                on the road to Development.

"Where's your house? Where do you live?
Arrey sa, can't you understand . . .
OK, OK. Where *did* you live . . . ?"
            What is authority without a quick temper?

The labor-contractor sits at a desk
with his rosters of names by age, sex,
caste, and names of villages they've
come from.

An earthen pot of drinking
water for his exclusive use,
his lunch bag, and his glittering motorbike
share the ampler shade of the only
　　　neem tree in the vicinity
his transistor-radio blaring away romantic
songs no one understands.

KIMBERLY M. BLAESER

Ice Tricksters and Shadow Stories

~ for Jerry

I.

Later that winter she began to hear voices.
No insistent whispers of conscience,
Not the teasing of her muse,
Voices of ice, ice voices.
Tinkling like wind chimes,
    the coated branches of trees,
Waking her again at night,
    banging and booming across the wide expanse of frozen lake.
Ice, a delicate porcelain,
    shattering with a hollow pop beneath her feet;
Screeching beneath the sled runners,
    mock pain echoing in winter silence.

II.

Her companions all deaf to the diamond poetry of ice
She, fearing the beauty, the coming of this new ice age,
Listened in trembling search to sounds become voices
Become words become shadow stories of ice.
Recalling the mystery of ice point,
    the temperature of equilibrium of pure water and ice;
Remembering the story, how ice woman froze the wiindigoo
    at just that point in the moccasin game.
Having sought herself that delicate equilibrium
    between recklessness and cowering,
Knowing truly how the balance of story sustains two natures,
    she began to imagine, ice shadows.

For Africa's ice plant, a trickster story:
    fleshy leaves covered with glistening crystals,
A suspended transformation, a metaphor for life,
    like the evil gambler frozen by ancient ice woman,
Like delicate ice needles, floating in midair,
    finding the circumstances to defy gravity.
Suspended herself, frozen in winter time, an ice floe
    locked happily in a glacial epoch,
Sustained now by the hypnotic voices of ice—
    trickling, tinkling, cracking, booming
Ice tricksters telling story
She began to hear.

III.

Hearing, too, at last,
    their sounding the metaphors of death,
In the trees, limbs enveloped in glitter,
On the ledge, spikes honed of crystal water,
Both incandescent, resplendent with their sun death
Ice capsules weeping their own doom, icicles crashing to earth.
Angry now, she skated madly by the moon's light,
Feigning indifference, ignoring the screaming sound
When her blades cut a fresh path across the hardened lake,
Believing somehow she was forestalling breakup, meltdown, spring,
Knowing human things like refrigeration and dry ice,
Believing in the science of Celsius and centigrade,
Thinking ice trickster to be of water and winter,
Subject to simple laws of time and temperature,
Forgetting temporarily the ice shadows cast by myth.

IV.

Then falling one night asleep or beneath the ice,
Finding herself pulled from dream or watery death,
To waken damp with memories of a silent ice woman.
Wondering had she been rescued or been condemned,
Wondering if she was human, or ice, or shadow,
Wondering if her voice sounded or was silent,
Wondering if her story was the present or the past,
Wondering if she was myth or reality,
Wondering finally, if perhaps they weren't the same,
At least the same, in that mysterious center,
  that ice point of consciousness,
  that place of timeless equilibrium
  where one begins at last to understand voices.

On the Way to the Chicago Pow-Wow

On the way to the Chicago pow-wow,
Weaving through four-lanes of traffic,
   going into the heart of Carl Sandburg's hog-butcher to the world,
   ironic, I think, landing at Navy Pier for a pow-wow.
I think of what Roberta said: "Indian people across the country
   are working on a puzzle, trying to figure out what I call
   —the abyss."
Driving into the abyss. Going to a pow-wow.

On the way to the Chicago pow-wow,
Laugh when I look down at my hands.
Trying to tell you, needing to hear you laugh out loud
   because the puzzle was made by madmen who want us all lost
   in the rotating maze.
I think my hands have stepped out of Linda Hogan's poem:
One wears silver and tourquoise, a Zuni bracelet and a Navaho ring.
One wears gold and diamonds, an Elgin watch and a Simonson's
    half-carat;
The madman's classic mixedblood, a cliche.
Together, laughing out loud at the madness. Going to a
pow-wow.

On the way to the Chicago pow-wow,
Thinking of home, I know we are driving the wrong way.
It's not Lake Michigan I want to see.
It's not Wrigley Field.
But there is no exit here to 113, no cut-across.
I think of Helen's cabin, sitting by the fire drying my hair,
   and Collin talking:
     "Sometimes you have to go in the wrong direction
     to get where you're heading."

Driving southeast, heading northwest. Heading home,
   to White Earth Lake,
   to Indian ball diamonds,
   to open air pow-wows.
Taking the Eden's, going to the Chicago pow-wow,
   on the way back home.

Absentee Indians

Used to think they were white.
They'd come
visiting Grandma's.
Big cars,
neat little
quiet
scrubbed-looking kids
in matching tennies.
Come from somewheres else for sure.
Sundays
or maybe just seeming like it,
and acting like a holiday too.
Absentee Indians.
Back for a memory
a fix if they could find it
get them through
till next pow-wow
sugarbush
funeral
next lonely.
Old Man Blues we call it,
emptiness bubbling up like a blister
ready to pop.
Ain't no cure for it
but home.

Now it's me returning
going visiting
making the rez rounds
like all the other absentee Indians.
A week to see my whole family.

Twenty-five minutes apiece each.
Picnic at Coffee Pot landing
fishing at Uddies
berry picking, sausage making,
one of every good thing squeezed in.
Hardly time enough
this trip
but making plans
next trip.
Litanies of family names,
river talk, hollows,
reciting hunting camps,
pine-pitch memories
what used to be.
Hoarding remainders
things never meant to be counted
like prayer breaths.
Searching some magic antidote
boiling pine boughs
some sequence of recall
twelve steps
to ward off homesickness.

"Twice a year I come
to see the folks," he said.
A city Indian
some relative from California.
"Summers I bring the kids.
Want them to learn about their heritage."
We used to laugh
when he said heritage
like every book on Indians
instead of people or tribe or life.

Ain't hardly laughing now.

March 1998: Seeking Solace

Mother, Auntie, Grandma, Marlene,
we believe you inhabit these lands.
Your spirit embedded here
blowing like Bass Lake breezes
across our fish-wet hands.
Pushing up moccasin flower shoots
along the Tamarack trails.
Casting before us scents
we know to be our relatives
cedar, pine, and sweetgrass.
Etching story words and pictures
in white-gray birch bark patterns.
Calling names in the language of birds
Nay-tab-waush, Alah-no-men
Gaa-waababiganikaag.

And we leave here now
dreaming White Earth dreams.
Scarlet flames of sumac,
soft green fronds of fern:
colors nudge dark edges of despair.
And we leave here now
bearing close, round images of home.
Of hummingbird's nest and family markers,
large brown Antell eyes,
twice delicate abalone vision:
Earth mounds like fallen breasts,
soft moss of women's cleft lives.
Hallowed here by wailing wolf orphans
voices form like dew at dusk at dawn
moist with treasure, hoarse with desire.

Night webs, filters of howling darkness,
catch and sift our dreams, feed us peace.
Woven labyrinth, source of warm rest,
your healing feather drips chip through,
melt deathly cold winter-ice loneliness.
Now lips in sleep move with prayer breath
ripple the soft down underside of ducks.
And we sign ourselves followers
of allotted land and lives;
And we sign ourselves followers
of Bunkers, Browns, Antells and Blaesers.

JENNY BOULLY

Selected footnotes from *The Body*

[58]   In the original production, Boully was positioned stage center, the vase contained lilacs, not violets, the hills spread out like fallen pears, and _____ was originally cast to play the role of _____ who, in the original production, entered on the cue of broken glass to ask if she would _____ him. The addition of black curtains, which replaced the billowing, transparent ones, was made in the year _____. Del Vecchio contends this is indicative of Boully's growing apprehension of _____. The change in the set design was intended to symbolize the changes made in the dialogue, as _____ would no longer be asking if she would _____ him, but if she was okay with just _____ing him.

[59]   Not the celestial body, but the cleaning agent, which was commonly used to scrub toilets and dislodge mildew from cracks and crevices.

⁶⁰ From her travel journal, written during the five years of her self-im-
posed "nun-hood":

> I tried to make myself pure by giving up touching myself, that part of
> myself that my mother used to call a turtle and then a clam. But there I
> was, under the blue mosquito net, blue, not unlike the color of my
> dreams. The cocks were crowing for morning and I began; I began having
> to start this dream over again. (Perhaps when the cock crows, it signifies
> only the crowing of the cock and nothing more. Perhaps the aubade is,
> in fact, only a convention. I should be so free.)

⁶¹ The dogwoods were especially lovely that year.

⁶² To this particular question, she always answered, "No comment."

⁶⁸ Actually, what she most desired was someone who would pay close attention to details — the type of person who would never misplace a comma or misspell a word, who would point out and love all those things she deemed lovable about herself such as the manner in which she wrote ampersands, the two freckles on her left hand, the golden highlights in her hair and other such trifling matters; secretly, therefore, she desired someone who might allow himself to be engaged in the world of platitudes, yet she always sought out men who liked to (o)pen the heaviest of books and read them whorishly, jumping from one author to the next, abandoning one for another, starting one and never finishing, forgetting the minute yet most important details and the names of characters, folding corners instead of using bookmarks, writing pretentious marginalia, pretending to have read certain books when engaged in cocktail-party-conversations, reading certain books only to be able to say they have read them and without want or love, etc.

⁶⁹ According to legend, it would rise from the bog on the night of a full moon in search of.

¹³⁶ The onset of puberty *would* mean the death of eternity: with menstruation, she would know that a month had passed; when it ceased altogether, she would know, for certain, that the years had elapsed.

¹³⁷ Even so, I go my own way, following the drifts of the hourglass, laurelled with lightning-blue bumblebees, at the foot of the lunamoth-winged sky, as on the bottom of the whale-born sea.

¹³⁸ The response from the great poet was written on a postcard:

> J: You've failed once more in that a good poem is never tidy —
> never let on that you went through great pains to get your lipstick just
> right; lines should break like kamikazes; you should be beautiful in your
> slovenliness; you should be enticing in your near-suicide.

[139] It was unearthed from its burial site and auctioned off three years later. The proprietor spoke rather vaguely of its contents: _____, _____, _____, and a used _____; he was, rightly so, disappointed, thinking that the box contained gold or jewels or money. Tristram, who could not stand for such ill use of the author's most dear of possessions, offered his life's savings in exchange for the chest and its contents: what he found were all the letters, among others, that he had composed to her; a photograph he took of the author at 24; her journals; a map of _____; an itinerary for _____; a moth-infested wedding dress sized 4; and a ticket stub to *The Real Thing*.

JACQUE VAUGHT BROGAN

Window

I have known something of terror,
and seen the bodies where
the chisel of long starvation

has exposed the underlying bones,
and here, the five women carved,
limb from limb, like stones.

For a long time the fear
was personal, dreams of my father
burning me in a kiln

even as my mother called me home.
Or, just looking back, finding
I have lived alone.

I haven't had to imagine
it—or you—
As if from the distance of a god,

we've seen the surprise of color
rise over the moon,
something blue, brown, and green

(with a swirling white mosaic) lift
majestically in the dark
as if something

utterly miraculous
must be being
shaped there—**Here**—

Stable

Here I am, the wild horse
in harness. Cold nights
of cruel roaming tamed
to needles, knitting, nagging.

Everyone must have known
how it would be,
but they wouldn't tell me,
the man with the dark eyes,

the old woman serving cake—
not even him, my handsome rider,
who trained me to trail his smell—
I thinking I was finally free

when everyone knew
that bride meant bridle.

from Notes from the Body

ii

for Sandra, who is having a hysterectomy

Through our bodies—
stories we just re-member.
                  Mishawaka
name of nearest town named
of Indian princess.
           Tapi Toppy
my own ancestor, Cherokee, we know not
the spelling of
           who still passed on
through her daughters this knowledge

        each stone is alive earth is alive

Spirit—we arrive like
       horses

           stand on our own
          so soon,

         never forgetting
             that grass
                  is
           milk,

           wind is moon
           menses
           in the making.

I call my friend.
Against doctor's
        orders, she is
        keeping one
                ovary.

One's enough
she says, to keep
her health
        cycling.

viii

Etymology 1816—Naming
the 19th State *Indiana*

> *India*: Skr. *sindhu* river, spec, the Indus
> hence the region of the Indus,
> > Sindh (by extension, with Greeks and Persians)
> > the country east of this.
> Applied to America or parts of it
>
> *Indies* orig. India with the ad-
> jacent islands, later called *East Indies*
> > (*West Indies*, which had come to be applied
> > to lands of the Western Hemisphere
> > which were taken
> > to be part
> > of the Eastern group.)
>
> > Spirit, and blessings, great mother
> > no air for my voice in those words
> not even logical
>
> > The Council Oak did not die
> > of old age. It fell apart, it ripped itself
> > wide open to witness the rings it had weathered.
>
> > She would have fed the ground again
> > with her body. And I try to dance with mine.

They must be coming, gathering they are
the feet of women, in which there are other
                rhythms, different logics,
who'll give the name back to this
we call St. Joseph River,
Notre Dame, Indiana,
New York, New World
taken to be part
of the Eastern group.

        What trees are left are talking
                blazing they are this autumn—
                with burning colors

        They say,
                this is the history of a mistake
                which they kept making
                after the mistake was known

ix

Fire Spirit

Somewhere, out there,
you are,
    scattered through the geo-
    graphy.

I need to open my eyes
carefully (full of care),

to the wind tickling the lake
        (coins of light are
            skipping
            on the waves)

and trembling the leaves
        (small ovations
        applauding
            each reddened apple)

and to wait—
    wait for the soul
        to climb out of the trees.

Notes from the Body—

Is it over between us, before it's begun?

We talk, several times daily,
           at great cost.

      Something spiraling between
           our vision—naked trees,
   gray light, flashing storms,
          reddest aspens
         of the fall

You're afraid of your job.
    I'm afraid of the world—

What tree, what sister,
        felled again
    whispered her last
    syllables this night?

        And did anyone hear?

My neighbor, pregnant,
    and with a two-year old child
    was murdered.
Someone tried to break in
    to my house, twice in one week.
(My children were asleep—with only
    one staircase: no escape.)
I could go on.
        I try to go on.

Listen: the air is hurting
like a person
who misused the once sacred
tobacco

Water is phlegming
like a person
with too many years
of too many medicines

If I can't say this
to you, whom I know best
of all, how can I speak
of it, of us, at all?

Today, *that* man was lonely,
on my street,
dressed in a heavy overcoat,
hiding something cheap—

and the river, St. Joseph's
only looked clean from the street

Children are dying
at 74 degrees heat
from hypothermia (starvation)
a whole continent is dying
(global warming) Antarctica

And we've all lost our names.
And the map stays the same—
                        it says,

In every war
      someone always rapes a corpse,
      someone pisses in a flagging
            mouth
      someone puts out a cigarette
         in a frozen eye
      someone always cuts out a tongue
         not knowing why

Is it over between us,
before it's begun?

I never bore your children
      nor danced in the sun-
            light upon the waters
Austin, Oahu, wherever—

      this spiral, this spiro-
            graph, even spies of my own

      keep nudging me, saying
            separate
      and not because I've quit loving you—
            aspen smells
            flannel voice
            leathered whispers
            silk and skin—

      but because I'm becoming afraid
      of just how much
      I really am
            learning
            to hate

STACY CARTLEDGE

inertia

what is lost (in memory) is all
but that which scars

searingly enough to shape.

you want to know why, what
held me back—
i was lost. i became lost within you.

and there was no thought
for poetry, not beyond which music
could be made by our bodies, soft, your sighs;

the words meaningless but with the weight of truth.
i said them slowly, precisely.
they had the heft of silence long-kept,

and the weight of the words slipped over us.
i felt them slide past our smooth skin,
catching on nothing . . .

it seemed a natural thing to touch your hair,
to stroke my fingerprint across your cheek.

we whispered lines as if from a script,
finding the portrayals that would lead us

into moments of late night, sitting in cars, waiting
for windows to fog, ruminating the senses.

my ear to your breast;
and in that moment i listened to your heart

and found you solid, alive; arms reaching around,
a moisture on the skin, damp warmth

and the breath, played in relief against
the quick thumps of your heart, pounding.

i close my eyes—dreams, like catching stars in a net.

divine comedy

i wake to a room blue with predawn
and a premonition.

i met your parents only once, perfunctorily
before our second date, in the same low room of your split-
level where six months later we listened
to the planets move resoundingly around us.
so only because it is a dream do i
recognize them, and they me. they reunite us . . .

i lift and hold you as if before a threshold
and, with hair black now, you make me promise
to buy you presents, your studied approximation
of archetypal girlishness a sure sign
of subcutaneous happiness—a fact
i realized, lumberingly, only too late:
you had needed something from me.

at once i know i'll rush to the bookstore, for Dante, for the *Paradiso*;
or, if that's too much a step ahead, the *Purgatorio*; either
thus defines our previous relationship by the *Inferno*
our dissolution left with you.

but suddenly all this seems too right, too
easily found; and this my grasp
is on is something untenable: and it is loosening.
struggling to save some sliver, the dream begins again—
—but this time, when i find your parents, they tell me
you are dead.
        suicide, of course, years ago.

and this, eleven years after
that afternoon we heard Holst
and let no reason not to become a reason for—
an awe-struck moment of definition,
replete with rug burns.

evanescent

in the same way you hear the swooping call
of the red-tailed hawk, constantly curving
the acute angles of flight,

there is the bubbled rush, during your dive,
of the ear's channel flooding, filling,
as you break the liquid and glide

through the squared web of light, a tunnel
patterned by algorithms of crest and trough
rippling the surface, dancing mesmerically,

flitting mathematical purpose.
water is full of waves, both those and light;
add to it music, the tension breaking

the surface and issuing then, while parting
light from light and crest to crest,
the equivalent in air, a rolling movement

spreading and equalizing so the effect is negligible
everywhere but locally, and there only briefly (for
there are waves in time as well); and as the light

shifts, second by second conforming to the changing
path of the hawk, time becomes visible:
its beauty, as yours, owed to its passing—

codex
(a discourse)

the insistence on death—the stillness that comes complete
outside time, nothingness is as much matter
as it is death as much as matter is life.

consider the abstraction of touch: remember
    when we felt the car lift us
    in its search for traction—the unreality
    of collision, hardly a crunch, just a toss
    like the toss of the butterfly
    we found that time, grounded by wet wings.

    i wrote a poem about that too.
    about how we brought it into the car,
    and turned up the heat to dry it,
    and turned up the heat on ourselves.

    i thank you now
    for your confessions that day,
    the ones that made me see your smile
    as turning on me. that made me say i wouldn't
    take it anymore, your past, past—how much
    could we have had then, ten years ago?
    it did break me.

    but still, this year
    i went to your house for thanksgiving.
    your new house, your
    married home.

the landscape has no name.
the dirt does not know the stone it cradles, to sink
that far—eyes waned down to windows, accepting
the cold a moment, until
breath returns.

consider the abstraction of smell: remember
the differing scents of our bodies;
i catch the breath of laundry
clinging to the smoothness
of your arms, your hands, your belly,
i feel the roughness
of the skin above your breasts,
somehow less pale.

a drowsying smell, when i put my cheek
upon you—its taste was light,
and breathing it was all there was of air.

how many poems have i written for you? i know you
told your husband how the last one
came about, those final nights before
you moved into the city with him.

i've watched you grow more
cynical, more so even than me. i suppose that's why,
when i told you what i did
yesterday, i felt instantly
like the worst kind of poet—a Romantic.

do you believe me when i say
i felt i owed it to them, that they see
what i'd written while they sat
holding each other before me?

or do you believe me,
and think it mawkish?

the motif of "I" is a form of interference.
god could be the echo of the universe's
beginning—a radiation homogenized throughout.
the only point of view not tainted by perspective.

and consider the abstraction of sight: remember
    the photograph i took of you playing cello,
    with the extended exposure so that it captured
    not one instant, but movement. the arcing
    bow, the swiftness of arms; legs
    parted, tangling hair.
    and was it that day, or another, when you cut my hair? again,
    it was after you'd said *no more.*

    but it was you who kissed me,
    grabbed me with the hair still sticking
    and itching on my neck, as you sat
    on the sink and were desperate
    and i dug my fingers in and the heat off you covered us,
    drove us,
    like the night of your brother's birthday years later,
    when i ended it by wanting,
    by assuming, more.
    the last time i felt you warm
    against me.

    this, seven years after i thought
    i'd already kissed you for the last time,
    back on that summer day when i came to your empty house
    for lunch, sweating from the hot warehouse
    where i'd thought all day,
    and angry, so angry at your past
    and we didn't eat, no,
    you also were angry, and we were angry together,
    and you also were sweating, and we were angry and sweating
        together,

and you lay naked under me for the first time—and i shook.
i looked at you
and loved you. i was nervous, afraid
to abandon my boxers, so
you touched me through them.

and then the day of the butterfly,
and you held my hand; a gesture
i'd thought forgotten. if i hadn't
remembered perhaps there would've still
been a chance. but then the night my car
burned, and you wouldn't speak to me anymore.

and the sad thing is, i'd just finished,
when i drove the three hours up for thanksgiving, i'd just
    finished
correcting again the first poem i wrote for you,
a revision i thought proved
i no longer needed you. it was about
the butterfly, that one with heavy
wings, that one i found under the dash
after our fight and your departure,
about how i gave lift to it, gestured
it out of my hand,
and watched it fall.

MICHAEL COFFEY

Lawrentian

Assonance at every instance, or every other.
Offal odor, effable—the less for it—
leaving autumn eager and overrun.

Oblation, time of need; gourd-like
and engorging. Pearls, purses full,
gulp up awesome dishes of a sound.

Of a fissioning and the pound of it
burst finally, plum-bruised and stewing,
the low sun brown with bees.

A Fact of Language

Despair
is raped. Dies. Spars idea.

Sides rap. Raps. Pair a dice.
Sad rips, sea. Seas rip, rap.
Rap dies.

Rap said: ear, as paid.
Dip air.

Rid apes, sir. Ride.
Air sped, a spider. Air raid.
Peas, seas, sad as pies. A pier.

Dire, asp. A rise rises.
Drips repaid, a spread, said:

Red, a air. Spare
sped as id, aspire.
Said per and dire.

Aspired, as ride is.
As pride is.
Is praised.

Melville on the Beach

Pounding, again, assurances of the surf,
a ceaseless splash of water worrying
black rocks back to depths and down . . .

The heaving, sloshing lots
of urgencies renewed, ocean's
renewal, storm-heightened
by small squalls of protest mustered
at the world's stoniness, the brass . . .

And then a relenting, an easeful
backing to a steadier state,
rhythm's assertion
that all is plain in water and air,
and the sea is full of syllables.

Dad's Shoes

He's gone now, and so
poems catch you up with
what you know—the deaths
of fathers, in this case.

But the basement doesn't
know, in this house he built
for twelve grand in 1960.

There his seabag hangs still—
unperturbable canvas
cracked, deflated, coarse,
suspended from a rope
wound somewhere in the war.

Scattered behind the furnace,
beyond burst cartons of books,
a golf shoe and a forlorn
boot, its two rows of eyelets
curling away, spilling
a complexity of laces, yellowed,
untugged for years.

An abandoned bread box in the corner,
black with a peeling floral
decal, sits atop an old
nightstand thickened with
spilled paint and sloshed compounds,
relegated, both, to storing

Ideas of Order

Repeated rage poles portioned were word by word clear
uttered phrases stirred sea, sea; wind we, except its its its
distances cloud colored Fernandez
walked town tilting no coral enchanting

end that that deep
the the the the the the the
dark turned ever-hooded, ghostlier

water-walled to world keener knew voice
mastered like knew however wholly
air oh world, order been voice outer medleyed mimic
of of

or
among glassy water water water
her waves this ours
acutest motion ourselves heard only
origins

Theatrical pale Ramon never made
why alone zones for measured maker without whose
night descended mind
atmospheres

even if
formed, fluttering, dimly-starred
what what what
our

her mask grinding gasping
tragic-gestured more hour
was was was was was was horizons
made portals heard

beyond
constant cry caused constantly
a cry although empty, heaped plungings fixing me
wind

lights fishing fiery
toward voice vanishing, yet
body body
artificer

alone
anchor
we
fragrant

merely because for many
all genius it may be maker
since maker's not not not
air

she she she she she she
rose
and and and
spirit, beheld

song song song sang, boats
deepening but by which sleeves, bronze,
shadows sound there if sounds in
sight
sound
night
place
blessed

arranging speech, summer demarcations
heaving sing words
have sky more meaningless, mountainous
solitude

said
understood, inhuman, single
tell
veritable ocean sought self, sky

a striding
a sunken
emblazoned
Ramon

SEAMUS DEANE

Smoke Signals in Oregon

Like the Indian in the photoless forest
Which crowds this muffled house,
Fear flits through me leaving
Imagined tracks in the soft
And sucking mud that swarms
In the rain outside my door,
While I wait for the real footstep
To clump on the steps and
For the murderer of my sleep
To shudder into the stiffened core
Of the house like a shadow-stabbing
Presence looming on firelit walls
And vanishing up quickly
As my moving lips close.

Pour out the glimmering coal
That slides off the shovel
In a composite crash and
All night watch it turn to
Flame in soft internal shudders.
In the scuttle the coal crumples
Under my pale face, I see
My origins open as briefly
As a sleeping eye in the
Loaded head of a snake.
With that comes the fear in the belly,
Snake slabbed on the arm, tomahawk
On the rising scalp, the fire
A thick growth, roots antlered.

Death. Could it be so quiet?
It mows over my skin as stealth
Parts the lisping grass,
It darkens in my eyes
As cold grieves in the stiffening
Water, it enters the room
Behind my shoulder and shuts
The door into the wall forever.
The smoke roots hesitate on the coal,
The tree warps in the soaring chimney,
And through the wide American night
The ghost totem mounts in a pillar
Of vague faces; the First Faces;
Faceless; smoke signals for fright.

Migration

Someone is migrating.
He is going to the fifth
Season where he can hear
The greenness planning its leaves
And the landbreaks and the water
Co-ordinating the moment of foam.
He is going to seek his parents,
Looking in the history of their bodies
For what he inherited. He is migrating
Out of his nativities,
His tongue still undelivered, waiting
To be born in the word home.

Shelter

Two years after one war,
And some time before another,
In nineteen forty-seven,
Came a heavy fall of snow
That drifted over the slab
Of the air-raid shelter roof.

Before, there had been an infinite
Summer, full of the pock
And applause of the false spirit
Of cricket. As our reproof,

Came the savage winter
When the boiler burst
And the water in the lavatory bowl
Shook. To tell the truth,

I could see nothing wrong.
Winter was like Russia
At last and the war-games,
Ice-pointed, less uncouth.

Perhaps I heard my mother
Dreading the thaw and frost.
When I turned to look, though,
She was at the fire, face aloof

In concentration. Doing the sums
For food and clothes, the future
In endless hock. I went out
To the air-raid shelter roof

To throw snowballs. The whole summer's
Bowling went into my swing
And I flung them splat on the wall.
Damned winter. Her spirit, unsheltered,
Made me numerate at last
And, since forty-seven, weather-proof.

History Lessons

~ for Ronan Sheehan and Richard Kearney

"The proud and beautiful city of Moscow
Is no more." So wrote Napoleon to the Czar.
It was a November morning when we came
On this. I remember the football pitches
Beyond, stretched into wrinkles by the frost.
Someone was running across them, late for school,
His clothes scattered open by the wind.

Outside Moscow we had seen
A Napoleonic, then a Hitlerian dream
Aborted. The firegold city was burning
In the Kremlin domes, a sabred Wehrmacht
Lay opened to the bone, churches were ashen
Until heretics restored their colour
And their stone. Still that boy was running.

Fragrance of Christ, as in the whitethorn
Brightening through Lent, the stricken aroma
Of the Czars in ambered silence near Pavlovsk,
The smoking gold of icons at Zagorsk,
And this coal-smoke in the sunlight
Stealing over frost, houses huddled up in
Droves, deep drifts of lost

People. This was history, although the State
Exam confined Ireland to Grattan and allowed
Us roam from London to Moscow. I brought
Black gladioli bulbs from Samarkand
To flourish like omens in our cooler air;
Coals ripening in a light white as vodka.
Elections, hunger-strikes and shots

Greeted our return. Houses broke open
In the season's heat and the bulbs
Burned in the ground. Men on ladders
Climbed into roselight, a roof was a swarm of fireflies
At dusk. The city is no more. The lesson's learned.
I will remember it always as a burning
In the heart of winter and a boy running.

JOE FRANCIS DOERR

January Thaw

Green as mistletoe in chinquapin trees
That lined the two-lane into Arkansas,
2 kids rolled through the January thaw—
For Whom the Bell Tolls rested on her knees
As she read aloud to him while he steered
The '40 Ford down old Rte. 66
To Hot Springs (off State 7) where they shared
A honeymoon kiss between motor checks.

Toltec Mounds near Little Rock, Heavener's
Rune Stone to the west, & Cahokia
North & east, formed a mystic triangle

That cradled every thought they, as lovers,
Would breathe in passion to say *Make me a
Child* . . . How futures begin to commingle.

Star-crossed

The last time around the prospectors freaked—
Afraid the desert would melt into glass.
Some hurried burros through landscapes that cracked
In the heat, & brother Helios
Burned holes in the heads of meteorites
That showered like Perseids through the dross
& filings: ice-smelt leavings of the comet's
Wrenching glans. Others were not as remiss.

One prepared for the coming disaster—
Plucking his beard in a parched arroyo;
Nailing himself to a Joshua Tree.

A deputy sheriff, not long after,
Found him laughing in a grim falsetto
Half-ass crucified, his hammer hand free.

Sestina for the Birds

We sit on the porch swing
and listen to the mockingbird
while April drinks the rain
just starting to fall
in long and sodden whispers
around the hedges.

Some wrens in the hedges
chirp like the chains of the porch swing
while we speak in whispers.
The spry mockingbird,
in whistles that rise and fall,
serenades the rain.

In an eavesdropping rain
of tiny blossoms, the hedges,
bustling with wrens since fall,
shake near the porch swing.
A wren scolds the mockingbird
and our dry whispers.

Giggles rise from whispers
as we weather her chilly rain
of ire. The mockingbird
buzzes the hedges,
and then lights on the porch swing
chain as blossoms fall.

Who would care should we fall
from grace in a hail of whispers
sitting on this porch swing
mocking the wren's reign
over her brooding hedges?
Would the mockingbird?

Head cocked, the mockingbird
leaves the chain. His wings rise and fall,
shrugging as he hedges
our bet with whispers.
He lights on a branch as rain
drenches the porch swing.

The porch swing is empty. The mockingbird
Bathes himself in the rain. Wren feathers fall:
Whispers and curses rattle the hedges.

A Piece of September

~ for Cat

Rain falls, and the lull between each raindrop
is time enough to hear you whisper "*Still.*"

There's no mistaking (although you are not present)
your voice, your breathing as the night unravels from within.

Thunder shakes the windows and a kind of vision,
kaleidoscopic through the beads of fallen sky,

breaks through the rattling pane with familiar passion
and wraps me in a tenderness I cannot disembrace.

Your love (I'm sure of it) envelops me in strata, worries
my confusing distance in a pristine nacre aglow

with a smooth, a shining iridescence that comforts
at a time when nothing comforts, a comfortless time

when all is indecision, rank deception
and disorder; storm clouds whirling, anything but still—

it worries my condition as one might sit and worry
the solitary spark from a cold, unyielding stone.

Yet there you are. Yet there I feel you, wrapping
sheets of so much tender mercy, sheets

of love and lovely worry, giving way to
the simple beauty of the worried pearl of love.

KEVIN DUCEY

Dien Bien Phu

The danger of dualist religions . . . is potential reversion to polytheism, to multiple and local gods, always a threat to Imperium. What follows in the name of the Word is Crusade, Auto-da-Fé, religious war . . .
                                    —*A Gathering of Proper Names*, Brooke Bergan

1.

He had gone
(one chieftain to another)
carrying his flintlock.

The secret service agents
hadn't noticed until
he was finishing
the nickel tour of
the East Wing.
                The French
called them Meo, or sometimes
Yeo—they being so unprepossessing
they didn't bother to
correct the name.

2.

A river winds through
the fortress and at night
during the siege
we could always go down
to trade with the Greeks.
How else
to maintain this uneasy war?

              Ten thousand
deserters have settled here
this narrow zone
of the Scamander or Nam Yum.
They've put up tents, dug
caves, sell food
from the black market—stuff
we can't get up on the walls.
Many of us still in retreat
from Stalingrad, avoiding
an interview with Weisenthal.

3.

The Vandals beyond the Rhine
were largely runaway slaves, dispossessed
freemen, seniors
unable to afford
prescription drugs—
Rome had it coming.

The old poet implied things
might change and ended
under a helmet on the walls
of Tomis on the Black Sea.

           His sergeant:
           Those hooligans out there, pal,
           don't care much for your poetry—
           They zooming round in them
           shaggy pony chariots (celts?) with
           .50 caliber mounted on back. Go
           tell it to the Geats.

(Though Ovid did
grow fond of the people of Tomis,
learned their depraved
tongue and before he
died wrote a few poems in that
Greekish.

> "You gotta live w/
> yr people
> as well as yr ghosts."

            She liked
these American things we sold
out of the shop
on Steinentor Strasse. We
went for a drink
across from the LälleKönig.
I love you Americans, she said.
You're so happy; no
sense of history.

4.

The back of the panel truck
rattled open at the farmers' market
in Minneapolis and the press
of Hmong shoppers
pushed me forward. The truck
was full of some fresh, green plant.
Something I'd never
noticed before, long stalk, with
single leaf—shaped
like an ancient spear-head. They
were tied in bunches and the people
all around me waved their dollars
shouting out their need.

Was it ceremonial? I tried to imagine
an American plant I'd desire as much.
A French-fry? The particular is
what you eat. The old
cheesemakers of Gloucestershire
can say which side of the hill
brings the best milk.
               (Though
cheese was not always so sedentary—
it was Odin's food, the nomad's accident
of milk
carried from the Rhine crossing to
Augustine's city.
               Only
here could someone say, "I don't care
about food." Or, as the meat inspector
said on resigning: I don't care
if it is irradiated, it's still shit.

Homo Habilis: The Tool-Maker

Praise the world to the angel, not the unutterable world;
you cannot astonish him with your glorious feelings . . .

—R. M. Rilke, *The Duino Elegies*

I saw a wooly rhinoceros yesterday
and we chased it down to the Stop'n Rob.
Edmond killed it, but we were too far
from the cave to get it back home
before nightfall and the hyenas.

We give each other drill bits
for Christmas. We don't really like
each other, but a tool is always
appreciated. A pack of angels
from the main office came down—
wanted to see how things were working
out. How we were getting along.
They ignored Edmond and his
fancy talk about astronomy, but they
fluffed their wings over my new drill bits.
"Atta boy," they said. "Nice tool." So we
showed them what we'd been making.
Carol brought out her toothpick; Sy,
his business card holder. The angels
nodded to each other
making marks in things they called "books."
Then Susan had to wreck it all. She told them
of the death of her child—the little girl
we were all so fond of and
the terrible accident of her death.
"This sorrow is my tool—sharpened
so hard and close to my heart,"

she said to the head angel.
"I don't need a stone to sharpen it,
this blade never grows dull. It is with me
always, never far
never far from my hand. Do you see?
Do you see its fine, sharp edge?" The angels
shook their heads. Closing their books,
they said, "here is one we don't know.
How quick it cuts, how sharp the blade." They backed
from our cave as if afraid. At the door, the last one paused,
his wings, we now noticed, looked a little worse for wear,
"from here out," he said, "you suckers are on your own."

Heretic

Immediately after we
condemned the last
of the heretics I
went downstairs to catch
the early train home.
The subway was crowded
and as the train lingered
at the platform I
thought of the white
blindfold tied 'round
the old man's face as the
judgment was read. I like
to see the children dancing
between the soldiers' lockstep—
like those tiny clock figures serving
attendance on the hours. The train
pulls out and bangs along the
underground curves, reaching
into the mountain, coming into
blazing sunlight on the other side.
Mechanical time is not
to be mistaken for life's passage
any more than this apparition of my desire
(glimpsed in an old man's gasp of fear)
is the same as that flame
that once burned so clear.

Lamentations

Homage to Vallejo

The ice-cream truck sings the little
song of my death. In a cloud
the Lord in his anger clothes
the daughter of Zion. In the pocket
of an old jacket: lint, handkerchief,
death. I have beaten death with a shovel
and a rope, though my death has done
me no harm. Still, it remains,
undismayed. In Pennsylvania,
the car noses its way through the fog.
Even after my death is dead I
went on beating it; tomorrow,
remembering all the times I carried
it, cupped in my hands, blowing
warm breath over its beaked little face.

Wim Wenders Versus the Wolfman

Desire is an engine of metamorphosis

The blind man sets Frankenstein's monster down
with a cup of coffee and a cigar—
though the monster is skittish
and flinches when the old man strikes the match.

Wenders' Angel falls to earth
picks himself up and walks over to the kiosk.
His first desire as a mortal:
a cup of joe and a cigarette.

Angels are monstrous
and we desire them
though they bite back
with desires of their own:
Her eyes may be dark,
the needle a sweet
black nipple of sugar—
how good that road of dark change.

Boris Karloff, played by
William Henry Pratt, inhabited
the role of Frankenstein's monster so well
he could never shake it.
Children, dogs, and Hollywood agents
cringed away in horror
at the creature and his lesson.

We are only the clumsy servants
of desire. Blind and Mr. Magoo-like
we have the very thing of creation
seated in our kitchen while we struggle
with a cheese grater.
"Here you are. Let me cut you a piece of bread—
Oh! I'm sorry. The knife slipped.
Did it cut you, my big friend?
Let's wash that cut in this tub of bleach—
Wait, leaving so soon?
You haven't finished your coffee."

The angels of the Lord stop by
They are terrible
in their changeless desire.
They're on their way
to blast Sodom and want
a coffee and a fag. You don't smoke
and only have de-caf.
Surely, the Lord will smite you down—
if only you knew it.
        Your angels insist
they don't want any bread, so
you give them oranges—feeling
your eyebrows singe as they
take them from your hands.
In this fire, you recognize
here is something outside the human:
a fulcrum to move planets.

CORNELIUS EADY

Miss Johnson Dances for the First Time

When Ophelia met the water
It was a gentle tumble of a dance,
A mixed marriage of a dance.
The swans were confused.
She was a contradiction in terms.
She was, simply put, a beautiful death.

Not so with Miss Johnson,
A wheat field of a girl,
Who held her breath
As she cast herself on the dance floor
In a metallic blue dress

At the Grange Hall on Saturday night,
Holding onto a skinny mechanic

Who knew two steps
That could be shown in public.
It was like being pushed off the raft by her father:
The awful moment when the body believes in nothing.
How ridiculous her body looked,

How her brothers loved to remind her:
A wharf rat.
A drowned cow.

When Amelia Earhart met the water,
Assuming, of course, that she met the water,
Did the sea mistake her for a bird
Or flying fish?

In the awkward moment she belonged neither to sea nor air,
Did she move like Miss Johnson moves now,
Bobbing like a buoy at high tide,
Gulping mouthfuls of air
As her legs learn the beat and push,
And her blue dress catches the mechanic's pant leg
Like an undertow?

The Way You Do the Things You Do

Okay: my daddy wasn't what you'd call a model parent. He was stingy, and his life sometimes gave his jokes a nasty edge that didn't fit the punch line, like the time he and a Puerto Rican neighbor gave me a cup of dark liquid, named it Kool-Aid just to watch an innocent tongue spit wine.

This afternoon, as my father lies unhealed in the hospital, my sister pulls up the story of the winter she had to shame him into buying me a coat by going downtown to Woolworth's and lifting one off the rack. It had become clear to her that he wasn't about to do anything, and she got sick of watching my back slump in the wind.

Now she adds a piece of the story she's carried for years: how can she tell her brother how a father decides that a child isn't a part of his property? We both know he's wrong, my mother backs us up, and he'll claim the same later with my retarded brother, but it sets a soul to wandering.

Months after my father's death, I have a dream. My wife and I check into what should be a "good" hotel, except nobody's bothered to straighten up our room. The sheets are soiled and jumbled, the kitchen alive with debris.

As I call the desk to complain, I feel my stomach sink the way it does before one's about to talk to a mechanic. Why, I think to myself, *do they think I have this coming? What did I do to deserve this?* What did they read on my face that told them *he won't squawk?*

The Supremes

We were born to be gray. We went to school,
Sat in rows, ate white bread,
Looked at the floor a lot. In the back
Of our small heads

A long scream. We did what we could,
And all we could do was
Turn on each other. How the fat kids suffered!
Not even being jolly could save them.

And then there were the anal retentives,
The terrified brown-noses, the desperately
Athletic or popular. This, of course,
Was training. At home

Our parents shook their heads and waited.
We learned of the industrial revolution,
The sectioning of the clock into pie slices.
We drank cokes and twiddled our thumbs. In the
Back of our minds

A long scream. We snapped butts in the showers,
Froze out shy girls on the dance floor,
Pin-pointed flaws like radar.
Slowly we understood: this was to be the world.

We were born insurance salesmen and secretaries,
Housewives and short order cooks,
Stock room boys and repairmen,
And it wouldn't be a bad life, they promised,
In a tone of voice that would force some of us
To reach in self-defense for wigs,
Lipstick,

Sequins

My Mother's Blues about the Numbers

My mother didn't get to keep
Much in her life. She tells me this story
Of the one time she hit big
On the numbers,
Guessed it, and hit it,
And then somehow lost it all
To my father and cousin.
Perhaps she trusted my father
Once too often,
And allowed him to pick up
Her winnings.
Maybe she fell asleep
A winner,
And woke up
To an empty wound
Of a hiding place,
A dream of greedy,
Prying hands
That wasn't a dream,
A crime too soft
To wake her up.

She's waited for years
For them to own up.
They'd laugh that laugh
That says: A woman
Can't prove nothin'.
My father's dead.
She's waiting now
For my cousin
To come forward,

But a man will never
Lift a woman
Towards the truth.
That's what these blues say,
That a woman must carry
To her moldering ground.

Dread

I'm going to tell you something
It's a simple fact of life.
If you're a young man in East New York,
Here's a simple fact of life:
If they don't shoot you with a gun,
They'll cut you with a knife.

I'm standing at the grave
Of a just-buried friend,
Staring at the fresh mound
Of a just-buried friend.
Don't know how it got started,
Can't see where it'll end.

Looked for a glass of water
But they gave me turpentine
You can ask for a glass of water
All you'll get is turpentine
I don't know why this life
Is like askin' a brick for wine.

I've lost eight friends already,
Who'll make number nine?
Lord, buried eight friends already,
Who'll be number nine?
I'd love to make plans with you, Sugar,
But I don't believe we'll have the time.

I sleep with the bullet
That didn't have my name,
Say *good morning* to the bullet
That didn't have my name,
So when my number comes up, baby,
It'll be the one thing you can't blame.

Why Was I Born? A Duet between John Coltrane and Kenny Burrell

So why? Asks the guitar(ist),
And the sax(ophonist),
A genius, a lover,
Side-steps the question,
Blows a kiss instead.
Then they both begin to speak
Like bourbon being poured
Into a glass at
Which bar? The eternal one
Bathed in the open light
Of the test pattern, the one
Where the phone booths
Are all functional, but
So? Better here than
Your shitty apartment,
His/Her scent on the
Bed sheets until wash day,
Perhaps longer. Better here
Than finding lipstick
On a bathroom glass, his
Brand of cigarette on the dresser.
Their melody is the touch you now wish
You'd never learned, the caress
Of fingers and breath
That promised, promised. What
Hurts is beautiful, the bruise
Of the lyric.

My Face

If you are caught
In my part of town
After dark,
You are not lost;
You are abandoned.

All that the neighbors will tell
Your kin
Is that you should
Have known better.
All they will do
Is nod their heads.
They will feel sorry
For you,

But rules are rules,
And when you were
Of a certain age
Someone pointed
A finger
In the wrong direction

And said;
All they do
Is fuck and drink
All they're good for
Ain't worth a shit.

You recall me now
To the police artist.
It wasn't really my face
That stared back that day,
But it was that look.

BETH ANN FENNELLY

Poem Not to Be Read at Your Wedding

You ask me for a poem about love
in place of a wedding present, trying to save me
money. For three nights I've lain
under glow-in-the-dark-stars I've stuck to the ceiling
over my bed. I've listened to the songs
of the galaxy. Well, Carmen, I would rather
give you your third set of steak knives
than tell you what I know. Let me find you
some other, store-bought present. Don't
make me warn you of stars, how they see us
from that distance as miniature and breakable
from the bride who tops the wedding cake
to the Mary on Pinto dashboards
holding her ripe, red heart in her hands.

Bite Me

You who are all clichés of babysoft
crawl to my rocking chair,
pull up on my knees,
lift your delicate finger to the silver balloon
from your first birthday,
open your warm red mouth
and let float your word, your fourth
in this world, *Bawoooooon*—
then, delighted, bite my thigh.
I practice my stern *No*. You smile,
then bite my shin. *No*, I say again,
which feels like telling the wind *No*
when it blows. But how to stop you?
This month you've left your mark on me
through sweatshirts and through jeans,
six-teeth-brooches that take a week to fade
from my collarbone, hip, wrist.
What fierceness in that tiny
snapping jaw, your after-grin.
You don't bite your teething rings,
don't bite your toys, your crib,
other children, or your father.
It makes us wonder.

Daughter, when you were nearly here,
when you were crowning
and your father could see your black hair
and lifted in his trembling hands
the scissors to cut your tie to me,
when a nurse had gone to the waiting room
to assure my mother *Just a few more pushes*,

when another had the heat lamp
warming the bassinet beside my cot,
then held up the mirror
so I could see you sliding out—
you started turning. Wriggling
your elbows up. The mandala
of your black hair turning and turning
like a pinwheel, like laundry in the eye
of the washer, like the eye of the storm
that was just beginning
and would finish me off, forever,
because you did it,
you got stuck, quite stuck,
and so, they said, I'd have to push
head-shoulders-elbows out at once.

And Lord did I push, for three more hours
I pushed, I pushed so hard I shat,
pushed so hard blood vessels burst
in my neck and in my chest, pushed so hard
my asshole turned inside-out like a rosebud,
pushed so hard that for weeks to come
the whites of my eyes were red with blood,
my face a boxer's, swollen and bruised,
though I wasn't thinking then
about the weeks to come
or anything at all besides pushing and dying,
and your father was terror and blood splatter
like he too was being born
and he was, we were,
and finally I burst at the seams
and you were out,
Look, Ha, you didn't kill me after all,
Monster I have you,
and you are mine now, mine,

and it is no great wonder
that you bite me—
because you were crowning
and had to eat your way out of me,
because you were crowning
and developed a taste
for my royal blood.

Latching On, Falling Off

I. When She Takes My Body into Her Body

She comes to me squirming in her father's arms,
gumming her fingers, her blanket, or rooting
on his neck, thrashing her mouth from side to side
to raise a nipple among his beard hairs. My shirt sprouts
two dark eyes; for three weeks she's been outside me,
and I cry milk to hear my baby—any baby—cry.

In the night, she smells me. From her bassinet
she wakes with a squall, her mouth impossibly huge,
her tongue aquiver with anger the baby book says
she doesn't have, aquiver like the clapper of a bell.
Her passion I wasn't prepared for, her need
naked as a sturgeon with a rippling, red gill.

Who named this *letdown*, this tingling upswing?
A valve twists, the thin opalescence spurts past the gate,
then comes the hindcream to make my baby creamyfat.
I fumble with one hand at my bra, offer the target
of my darkened nipple, with the other hand steady
her too-heavy head. She clamps on, the wailing ceases.

No one ever mentioned she's out for blood. I wince
as she tugs milk from ducts all the way to my armpits.
It hurts like when an angry sister plaits your hair.
It hurts like that, and like that you desire it.
Soon, soon—I am listening—she swallows,
and a layer of pain kicks free like a blanket.

Tethered, my womb spasms, then, lower, something shivers.
Pleasure piggybacks the pain, though it, too,
isn't mentioned, not to the child, drunk and splayed
like a hobo, not to the sleeping husband, innocent beside us.
Let me get it right so I remember: Once, I bared my chest
and found an animal. Once, I was delicious.

II. First Night Away from Claire

I forget to pack my breast pump,
a novelty not in any shop
here at the beach, just snorkel tubes,
shark teeth, coconut-shell bikini tops.
Should we drive back? I'm near-drunk
from my first beer in months. We've got
a babysitter, a hotel room, and on the horizon
a meteor shower promised. We've planned
slow sex, sky watch, long sleep.
His hand feels good low on my back,
tracing my lizard tattoo. And he can help—
he's had quick sips before—so we stay,
rubbing tongues, butter-dripping shrimp.

Later, he tries gamely, but it's not sexy,
not at all—he needs to suck a glassful
from each breast. The baby's so much better.
He rests. *It's hot*, he says, *and sweet.*
We're tired. We fall asleep.
I wake predawn from pain.

Those meteors we forgot to watch—
it will be thirty years
before they pass this way again.

III. After Weaning, My Breasts Resume Their Lives as Glamour Girls

Initially hesitant, yes,
but once called into duty,
they never looked back.

Models-turned-spokeswomen,
they never dreamed they'd have so much to say.
They swelled with purpose,

mastered that underwater tongue,
translating the baby's long-vowel cries
and oozing their answer,

tidal, undeniable, fulfilled.
For a year, they let the child draw forth
that starry river, as my friend Ann has termed it—

then, it was time, stopped the flow.
They are dry now, smaller, tidy, my nipples
the lighter, more fetching pink.

The bras ugly as Ace bandages,
thick-strapped, trap-doored,
too busy for beauty—

and the cotton pads lining them
until damp, then yeasting in the hamper—
all have been washed and stored away.

So I'm thinking of how,
when World War II had ended,
the factory-working wives

were fired, sent home
to care for returning soldiers,
when my husband enters the bedroom

Aren't you glad? he asks, glad,
watching me unwrap bras
tissue-thin and decorative

from the tissue of my old life,
watching, worshipfully, the breasts resettle
as I fasten his red favorite —

Aren't you glad? He's walking
toward them, addressing them, it seems—
but, Darling, they can't answer,

poured back into their old mold,
muffled beneath these lovely laces,
relearning how it feels, seen and not heard.

IV. It Was a Strange Country

where I lived with my daughter while I fed her
from my body. It was a small country, an island for two,
and there were things we couldn't bring with us,
like her father. He watched from the far shore,
well meaning, useless. Sometimes I asked
for a glass of water, so he had something to give.

The weather there was overcast, volatile.
We were tied to the tides of whimper and milk,
the flotsam of spit-up, warm and clotted,
on my neck, my thigh. Strange: I rarely minded,
I liked the yogurt smell trapped beneath her chinfolds.
How soon her breath bloomed sweet again.

She napped, my ducts refilled
like veins of gold that throb though lodged in rock.
When she woke, we adjusted our body language.
How many hours did she kiss one breast or the other?
I told her things. She tugged my bottom lip,
like sounds were coins beneath my fascinating tongue.

We didn't get many tourists, much news—
behind the closed curtains, rocking in the chair,
the world was a rumor all summer. All autumn.
All winter, in which she sickened, sucked for comfort,
a cord of snot between her nose, my breast.
Her small pillows of breath. We slept there, single-bodied.

Then came spring and her milk teeth and her bones
longer in my lap, her feet dangling, and, rapt,
she watched me eat, scholar of sandwiches and water.
Well, I knew the signs. I held her tight, I waded out,
I swam us away from that country, swam us back
to my husband pacing the shore, yelling and waving,

in his man fists, baby spoons that flashed, cupping suns.
It was a strange country that we returned to, separately—
strange, but not for long. Soon, the milk stops
simmering and the child forgets the mother's taste,
so the motherland recedes on the horizon,
a kindness—we return to it only at death.

KEVIN HART

Praying for the Dead

And in the church, silence.
The beautiful dead
Assemble: they creep

From chalices, the choir,
Gold candlesticks,
And hang above the pews

Like clouding breath.
Conjured by hymn and ritual
They glow, human,

Exhausted by the earth.
They waver like small hot flames
Impatient with the little we have to say.

For them, everything is lucid,
Now finally released
From the tangle of their lives

And each doubt cancelled.
They rise and dissolve like incense—
The night sky's waning lights

Are beckoning them home.
They will be taken for shadows.
They will be blamed for everything.

Some nights they will be
Smoke above the river,
Some nights

The cold worlds of the icons.
Theirs is the silence
At the end of all our talk,

Their answer
To all our questions, all our hopes,
Wordless as the priest

Eating the bread and wine,
Or the simple crosses
Pointing downwards.

A Silver Crucifix on My Desk

Each day you wait for me,
Your arms
Raised as if to dive into my element,
Your bowed, precise body
Broken into the ways of earth. Someone
Has shrunk you
To a child's doll that I might understand
All that it is to be a man:
A simple cross
Where two worlds meet, a man
Caught there
And punished by the storm between two worlds,
A sword thrust into my desk
That tells me
With each new morning that the world
Will not escape
The world that we have made.
By evening
I no longer look your way, but watch
Your shadow
Steal toward my hand, I hear you talk
In the clock's dialect
And my pen
Becomes an ancient nail. How often
Have I turned from you,
How often
Have I tried to shrink you down
And wear you round my neck,
As safe
As any of the stars you made.

You stand
Amongst the things of this world,
Old letters, photos,
An ashtray and a wallet, the things
That come and go, but you
I cannot move.
Once,
I put you behind me, and all day
I felt your long, torn look
Upon my back. So you returned
To watch me
Answer letters, light cigarettes,
And place my books
Beneath your feet. Each year
I grow
Toward your age,
A face moving to a mirror,
I measure
Myself against you, a child
Beside his father,
But I go up and down, while you
Remain
Always above me, poised
With arms outstretched, ready
To dive
In this cold ocean
With its lost treasure,
Its gorgeous fish, all blind as jewels,
Gliding through the darkness.

Making a Rat

I forget everything, and make a rat.
With little ambition at first, an amateur,
I try a roof rat—grey, long tail, sharp ears—

But with a will that staggers the human mind.
For months I labour on those teeth, that jaw
With strength enough to gnaw through beams of wood;

For years on end I fiddle with those ears
That make the lowest noises stand erect.
I give up dinners, seminars and sex

To breed the things it carries in its mouth—
Those strains of typhus, rabies, fever, plague.
I give up sleep for weeks to make its eyes

That pierce the darkness as I slowly work.
All day the mind will multiply itself
Just dreaming of a whisker hanging right,

A foreleg muscle tensing for a leap.
My mother dies, my father turns to drink,
And churchbells grow threadbare warning me;

And then one day the postman brings a book
Wrapped in brown paper, without card or note:
One Hundred Reasons Not to Make a Rat.

I put in longer hours, buy classy tools,
But still the rat won't work. I'll try again—
This time a Norway rat, eight inches long,

And from today I'll get it right from scratch.
I have my knives, my books, a practised hand.
Don't worry about that, I'll get it right.

My Mother's Brisbane

My mother's Brisbane was a mess of frangipani and flame tree
Seen from the windscreen of her car
Travelling through suburbs whose names she could not say

It was odd nights that fell without the benefit of evening
While working on dresses for weekends she wouldn't see
And it was hours with nothing much to do

It was a city remembered from old migrant books
Something about eleven hills and thunderstorms
Something about the Walter Taylor Bridge

It was the *Tele* and the Ekka; it was thongs and togs;
It was a child with a heavy port
It was a monthly visit to the Queen Street Mall

Something to do with Tracey Wickham I remember now
And something to do with Kingsford-Smith
And Lady Cilento had a place as well

Boris the Black Knight was someone she had to live with
Though Wickety-Wak she didn't
And Pancake Manor she never saw or Bunya Park

But the humidity she felt
While bent over that Singer on a summer's day
Or puffing through a family afternoon at Fig Tree Pocket

And the westerlies she came to feel as well
As though she let the city enter her a little more each year
Until she gossipped about the ghost at Stanley Street

And once she saw a bearded dragon half asleep
Beside the pawpaw tree in our back yard
And grabbed a rolling pin and chased it down the drain

The Word

There is a word that's set out from my death.
I know it has already left my lips
Although I don't know what on earth I'll say

When that time comes. It circles round the world,
And some dark nights I almost think I hear
The lemon tree out back repeating it.

I know it took the whole of life to say
That single word, and though it might seem weird
I half-imagine it is large enough

For me to live in now, a word so big
I'd never notice it while reading hard
Or find it looking up a dictionary,

That word I say a dozen times a day,
A word that slips my tongue just when you ask,
A word my death will not confide in me.

MARY KATHLEEN HAWLEY

innocences

~ for k.

i have just installed a ceiling fan you say
as we cross the quiet park toward the lake
this is after you tell me of the american
in the chilean secret police
whose green eyes choose you when he says
who in this room knows sheila cassidy

across the city in another room they are
torturing sheila   she will live and write a book
about it   his green eyes choose you, la inocente,
twenty-one years old and two months in chile
your mouth opens and says i know her
so they will take you instead of luisa,
yolanda, or barbara, who would never have returned
no one knows if you will return
but first, the madres say, we shall have communion
because it is sunday
taking the bread you whisper to them
but no one can hear in the silence of waiting instruments

you think you will die but they release you unharmed
they are sometimes careful with foreigners
before fleeing you spend a night
in the home of the cia chief
he warns you against meddling in things
you know nothing about
your youth and passport will not always save you

this happened thirteen years ago and now
we have dined at pasteur
a vietnamese restaurant in uptown
we walk along the lake as birds darken the air
wheeling out over the waves

my innocence ends differently, i say
in peru when i am twenty with a secret
slinking through the streets of a desert slum
we set out for the parish after curfew
our plastic sacks clank heavily
with broken glass, nails, chunks of wood
we are stupidly proud of our weapons
we want to finish them behind thick walls
in the morning strikers can scatter them
on the road, puncturing the tires of commuters

as we pass through the empty market toward the parish
a squad car glides up to us, no lights
we are ordered over for questioning
now when only the church lies ahead of us
i remember my secret: union leaders are hiding there

the little game stinks suddenly of death
my knees lock, my mouth will not open
it is my friends, without the secret,
who lean in the window to explain:
we are three americans out for a stroll
we live in the neighborhood
we didn't notice the tanks

the police sputter this is no time for stupid americans
you must stay indoors until order is restored
we carry our bags gingerly as they shepherd us home

now as you and i walk and the sun
drops below Chicago high-rises
you tell me even a ceiling fan does little
without cross-circulation   we climb into your car
and la inocencia enters with us
returned to us by two stories
and the remembrance of first terror

bogotá 1

a tremor ripples   on avenida caracas   in the walls
a crowd gathers   is a curious tool   as the man is lifted
completed   from the trash;   like this

picture of another   dead man
photocopy   bleeding   through the newspapers
humming   the exchange rate

there is a daily parade of them
hands tied   we didn't   feet tied
placards around their necks: *homosexual   comunista*

in bogotá   monday   is cemetery day
incense burns   on streetcorners   prayers
bought and whispered   in bogotá   the dead are visited

upon us

in iraq

~ for kathy kelly

everyone knows in this smoldering street
that american people do not agree with such
destruction   for the first time
she is glad there is no power for
the generators, no broadcast
of americans at home with the war on tv
how they smile at the generals
how they applaud as bombs find their mark
how they approve when journalists
ask no questions

biological warfare, she says, is the name
we can give it now: the merciless bombing
of bridges, power stations, water supplies
so disease will spread unchecked
long after the bombs stop falling
as doctors work by candlelight
their operating theaters dark and useless
as the old and the young
learn the price of fragility

from jordan, when the convoy is loaded
with food and medicine for bagdad, the americans
will not let them take milk, nor infant formula;
they can strengthen enemy soldiers

at the peace camp on the border
as war draws closer, iraqis come with buses
to evacuate them   an elderly british barrister
decides to stay;   he will not, all six-and-a-half feet
of him, be moved from the spot   a soldier
comes to him, kisses him on the forehead
and with others lifts him gently onto the bus

she, who has been bruised by the police
of her country, thrown into paddy wagons,
handcuffed, stepped on and slapped—she marvels
at this tranquil grace in the desert
as aftershocks rumble the sands beneath them

the road the convoy travels is a military target
american officials say they can do nothing
to protect it from american bombs
despite the white crosses
despite the cargo of medicines
it is the only road
in america, network executives
decide the story of whether or not
an international relief effort will survive
american attack is "not news"

"you must understand," two iraqi fathers
plead with her, "we would never
have sent them to the shelter
we only knew it was deep underground,
had thick steel walls, was a place for our women
and children to wait out the bombing
do not let your people believe we would
knowingly send them to their deaths"
she wonders how they care what americans
think, those whose country launched
the heat-seeking bombs that snaked through air vents
to incinerate five hundred women and children

and why do these men take the blame?
as if they had painted canisters with skulls
and dripping blood, as if they had taken off
another country and flown safely above
the clouds to push a button, drop the death
of their families, flash a victory sign,
race back to a tented city

on a bombed street a small girl approaches
threads a thin arm about the woman's waist
smiles and tells her name while her brother,
a little older, hastens across the street to a shop
and returns, carefully bearing three tiny cups
of water   he offers her a cup of water as a gift
from the people of his country to the people
of hers, "because we all know that
governments are not the people"

the mammogram

poor breast pressed flat between plastic plates
like some dumb sandwich   now i see
you are so much beef
why didn't mother ever say
they would lift my breast to a slab
and smash it   for a good picture?

when i was nine i ran my hands
up and down the smooth trunk   disbelieving
its twin stains
would someday swell

at slumber parties
i failed inspections
held in a forest of new hair
nipples and small buds

this was my guilty dream   someday
a boy whose fingers loved the curve
of a salty leather ball
its soft weight   tight stitches
would cup my breast
would taste it

but now my breast is clamped to a machine
for new inspections   shadows on a plate
this happens after thirty
someone looks for the wrong waves
bad weight   spoiled meat

yet there is also this:
now   when his lips press
against my two girls
i know it is food i offer
it rots   but also breathes
flushes with good heat

we are meat   feeding on meat
we are animals moving by night
through forests of blood and bone

JOYELLE McSWEENEY

Interview with a Dog

After three nights on the mountaintop, the dog began to speak.
The night sky curved around to hear

miel, honey, mille, the thousand flours, mildly

What language is he speaking? He needs dog friends—

My sheep were nervous in the passionless state.
I'd made it halfway to the goldfields
when my vehicle burnt to the ground on its own.

when the SWAT team formed a diamond and sunk into the canyon
    floor.
Wedged in the dripping crevice, I watched the circles spread

knowing the right one by its soaring expense.

This is a great apparatus for the United States,
here in the Superdome. What created light?
My master's spoken word.

I've been so sick and sad about this dump forever,
making lamps for the Vatican of design firms,
accounting for, abluting,

parading outside the city wall with my crew of wild turkeys,
and my Map of the Waterholes, Lava Flows,
Dune Seas, Cinder Cones,

The Barque of a Million Years

I remember the first metal doorframe I came through.
My name would not be finished.
Patronym, my patronymic,

where did you think we were?
After a lively class on joints,
I climbed up to the stadium over the sea
and down to its oval floor.
Steep rows of white seats swelled.

The bright disk of a coin in my open palm.
The gilt head of my sister-prince, looking away,
drawing the extra light from day down to herself.

Her solar barque came circling overhead
zeroing in to dock.

Palm trees flipped like bones above the golfcourse.
Lightning still-framed the progress of the celestial St. Bernard
and the always restless king.

That king was me. *Open and heal, my brother-bank!*
leaving him behind, I called, *for it is better and more natural!*
Daybreak at the butter farm, dominion of horses.
Fetlocks, socks. Stripes on my sleeve, a bee there.
A face of bees assuming its solar features.

What you only *seemed* to do, I had to do.
I mean you, Peter, rock in my path.
My re-birth in rock, my two roots forced,
one diamond-bit down through the shelly layer.

I was my own vital stepping stone, under the aegis.
Everybody fought to fit through the astral gates.
My hair tangled in the blades and wrapped handles,
boot straps and sandal straps, hooves and ankles.

Get behind me. Jump

A Letter from Venerable Annapolis
Sister. I got up to go look at the beautiful woman.
She wore a striped and swimming shirt.
A sea wind ripped back every cover.
Cold cars of light rolled out on the island.
Light chose one wave and not another—

Mithras, *sol invictus*, invincible sun,
are you the protector of this empire? Or what?
I ask you from this city built on a swamp.
In the green arcades, the old deities are dying and rising
in their tennis whites, serving and falling.

I sent the elderly children out to throw onto the sea
the blossomy laughter of the pundits.
I have invented fustian again from scratch.
Let me be unto this world as the spinning jenny
as the pre-fab rifle.

Down at the Inner Harbor,
Myself, disguised, descending
the big white sightseeing boats and shiny water.

Space must be filled with food and flower vendors,
musicians, hammers, banners, fountains, fountainings
benches and plants must overflow the midblock plazas

I didn't pray, afraid, in all the carpenters and scaffolds
The Eucharist going on
The bells exploding with it

What is this color vision *for?*

King: To understand and love at the same time the victors
    and the vanquished like in *The Iliad*—
      God:—I guess I just want to be seen.

    I like the attention towards me. I like the activity. I like the noise.
    I like the people. I like the people who work there. I like the scenery.
    I like the schedule. I like the operations. They said I wasn't there.
    But I was there.

of course, all fires look the same up close.
the prisoners went free,
doves from a dovecote,

the heretics went scrambling through the tri-state,
the picked-over degrees of divinity
stashed in their packs. Brainchild,

they are still at large.
night has fallen. the stone lion
has flown up to the pillar over the square.

under the bull moon,
the train is leaving which will carry us into our fosterage.
daddy, pull me down from the train through the window.
griffin-sister, leap from my back.

What I Eat Is a Prayer

Then in the August of my twenty-seventh year,
naked except for my seaclogs,
I greeted an audience of piers.

After my dip, I came up covered
in salt and sand: hair tough as an angel's.
Who could disappoint me now among the so-coifed?

Disappointing menus for a banquet of twenty-seven.
The hostess cannot hear the hotelier, walls blow ope';
lousy with wallets and checkbooks, the air. Naked except for

The checks and the monies flapped like birds.
I partook of the seasonal activity
and caught a check in my hands—to myself from myself—

and was caught; I was smart and dumb.
I hadn't been clobbered in such a long time!
Now, shoved against the carpeted headrest,

I wondered at its cold and slender neck.

The nakeder I feel the happier.

Camp is over, and the children come out
wearing hats; the children are happy for each other,
each camp having been maximally appropriate.

The ocean grew gritty with proteins. I arose
and clomb to the yard with its spigot.
It looked up and blinked. Above, kite strings wrote
toing and froing was the same motion; tiny sighs above the halls
at the county airport; swung on tiny chains;
my father swathed me in two handtowels,

said *nexttime, swim in the sea.*

A gold thread falls from an eagle's towel
onto the beach. A gold face big as a quarter of the sky
looks at us with gold-milk tears in its eyes

and the gold girl goes on brushing the countryside
with a twig-broom big as a tree. When our competitor
finishes third, he approaches the throne

with a gold wheel of tillamook.

The Born Fetus

The born fetus is a born scientist.
Flips his dish. Tries to glean a tan
from the overheads. Among the corrugated
cardboard and six-ringed empties,
the born fetus shifts.

A fore- and future thought.
He exists at the edge of a harbor,
curled on a rock. Both leg and tail,
he is the rock that replaced the ship's deck
under pilgrims' feet, in the cold bay
or harbor of the mind, at the edge
of any ill-defined gulf

he leaves the land for water:
sinks. Fights his livid burka like a kitten
in a sack. The born fetus collects shed characteristics,
takes the meteorological view. Invited for remarks upon
this sweeping arm, this plume

2.

The born fetus lies in his crib.
Above him the op-art mobile swirls
like a complement of possible developments.
He stretches up a hand. The brain
nets and releases.

An almond's papery skin
imprints the fingertip
before the hand can reach—No almonds for baby!—
imprints on the throat. Throat tightens at the possible allergen,
subsides. Sigh. Almonds and olives in the next room,
cattle and cars in the next state, hands
of born fetuses across the globe at this moment:

He drags his hand through the air.
In the next room, navels roll from the table.
Delay—thud. Delay—countably.
Left gaping, the red plastic netting.

3.

A film parliament is convened in Rotterdam.
An attachment scrambles the interface; a fish parliament
convenes, a screen of swimming pixels, a string
of unrecognizable characters strong-arms the in box. Cream

sinks and swirls in the stock. A thready pattern
collects, it is familiar. A hand rakes the air
with grapes and coefficients, from the rotting cupolas
and colonnades the godly leap
into firemen's nets and tarpaulins.
Grope for croutons. The charioteer
leans back, and with the tip of his whip
tickles the chin of the horse pursuant

4.

The born fetus is a born calculator.
Throat folds shut then—pop!—it opens.
On the plush
carpet of sensation, on the changing table,
the snug crux of the dilemma.
Are there always two or is it ten to the

With the blue foam cushion to hold him in the chair,
in the wash of the operating theatre,
in the lush cocktyllic suite,
the born fetus swirls among swirls.

He assembles indicia, stacks documents
inch-high, a citadel of one-storey
structures, over which he squats and flies
in a hand-built fantasy contraption.

5.

Light slots the seam in the curtain and picks out each part of the room.
It takes the day. On the monitor,
the red pulse makes the same gesture
over and over
as if waiting to be recognized.

The born fetus contemplates the fault tree.
The debris field of the mind
receives the sweep of a green arm.
It is a gentle, quiet gesture.
There are no people here and nothing can touch it.

Then electron-sized scapelettes
pivot and flash up a crown of brilliant sparks:
the doorlock reads the roomkey.

6.

The born fetus is held in arms
which provide no stop against propulsion.
In case of catastrophe,

he's as good as lost. Seeds pack the closed rinds
that pack the stands and think it over. Nth to the Nth.
Formula for miles above.
The born fetus is translated,

easily, from time to time. Slots through the lobe
of the sky. Over the looped track
where cars race, over rivers eating

caustic ribbons in the land:
deep familiar patterns
in the corpus

callosum
of the tennis courts;
in the red native lace
of Valencia, California.

ORLANDO RICARDO MENES

Fish Heads

A glowing crucifix (five
flashing lights) atop the lobster trap,
a rosary of papaya seeds,
a clock like a flaming heart
that shudders every hour;
the heart speaks: "I thirst,
It is finished, etc."

The fisher's son, an acolyte,
sleeps cuddled up in his canoe
of mist, rocking like censer
or bell buoy. Child of the sea,
river, lagoon—Antillean *querubín*,
who drools rose water on the pillow,
commands dolphin and barracuda
to weave arabesques of crown, cross, and pike,
boats skimming with sails of flogged skin.
Inside a pelican's pouch he flies from island
to island, wreathing with rain-lilies
light houses, masts, and campanili.

In their shack of tamarind wood,
a chapel on stilts, the smoke of candles
vivifies fish heads (nailed to the wall)
to bleed, quiver, turn east at cock-crowing;
a procession of ants will then surrender
to the flames. Lye falls
from clouds of ash. Lenten night:
the resurrection ferns will again be lush

and green. Yesterday the sea was vinegary,
less brackish than customary for baptism.
Waves release rosaries gnarled
with bladder wrack that village youths
unravel to mourn another acolyte.
Fragrant as sweet plantain, three mulattas—
fishnet menders—sing a dirge in Lucumí,
pantomime the hammerhead's thrust
and thrash to sign the boy's martyrdom.

Yemayá, Lady of the Sea, spawned
without sin, light from darkest water,
spare the fisher's son, swaddle him with fish
guts, brood him under your manta wings.
That blinding aureole will forever
burn above your shark's-jaw crown.

Hair

Hair tells family secrets, like lips and skin:
my chestnut curls and waves that intractable
thicket—one month's tropical growth—
Mamá called *maleza de manigua,*
jungle scrub. *What will the neighbors think?*

Locked in the bathroom, I brushed hard
against the grain—pig bristles, nylon quills,
chrome needles, nothing tamed
my guava bush, not even the wire brush
Papá used for mange of rust.

I rubbed sores with Mamá's alcohol
and iodine (mixed in squirt
bottles to disinfect the house of ghosts).

Prune this wild boy, Mamá told the barber
as she pulled my hair, grimacing, red fingernails
drawing blood. Cajoling the cranky
pedal with grease, Luis *el barbero* pumped
up the chair he'd bought at a Hialeah

junkyard, strop stained by rain; *la barbería* squeezed
between a butchershop and cigar factory—
"America, Love It or Leave It" macramé nailed
above hooks where *viejos* hung canes, Panama hats.

I slumped angrily, shoe kicking foot rest,
hands clenched under white shroud, plastic Virgin Marys
scowling at me for hating Mamá. Luis thinned
the bush with toothed shears, straight razor hacked
outer growth as Mamá reminded him

my *abuelos* were Spaniards—her Catalan father's
eyes between gray and blue, Roman nose,
his brother's hair just like mine, curlier even.
Tío Octavio looked Semitic, Mamá said,
you'd think he was Henry Kissinger.

Fat and bald, back hairs brushed up like a cockatoo's
crest, Luis shook his head, eyebrows raised,
smiling like someone who's heard this before.
Any hair's better than none, señora, any hair.

Miami, South Kendall, 1969

Papá was hosing down our new silver
Grand Prix, I scrubbing muddy floor mats,
when seven boys rode up
our driveway, legs tommy-gunned by mosquitoes,
eyes gunpowder blue.

They formed a line, passing around
a furry bowie knife.
Go back to Cuba, the chorus taunted.
We hate the Spanish.

Indigo snake coiled about his wrist,
Marcus hissed, snarled, telling my father
to kiss his ass. *Besamacula.*

A fellow fifth-grader, it was Marcus who'd pounce
on me as I walked home from school,
calling me a dumb spic for saying *yellow*
like *jell-o*, bony arms choking, my mouth scrubbed
in dirt of dandelion and bitterweed.

I cried alone in my room, ashamed
for not hitting back, praying for Marcus's death,
fists pummeling the pillow; Papá warned
I'd grow up queer if I couldn't fistfight
like my younger brother Carlos, "little rooster."

The boys began to hoot,
make monkey faces, Marcus playacted
a lynching with the snake.
Papá charged, spraying water, shouting *I cole
de polís, foqui sanambambiches.*

Then all seven mounted their bicycles,
sprinting toward avocado
groves; some days later we found death's-
heads carved on the garage door,
our cat Tintín's head floating in the pool.

Papá sold the house at a loss, and we moved
to a bungalow off Calle Ocho,
our neighbors newly arrived refugees.

By 1971 Freedom Flights
were bringing hundreds of Cubans
each day, my grandmother Nena
among them; the Everglades dredged
for an expanding Little Havana,
políticos dreaming of
a Malecón on Biscayne Bay.

Stars and Stripes
flying from car antennas,
hate signs taped to windows,
Anglos fled to rural Manatee
and Osceola, some journeying
as far north as Alachua,
Apalachicola Bay, Blackwater River;
and County Line Road,
a strip of gravel and sticks,
the new border dividing
America from América.

Ars Poetica

After black motor oil whet the chinked blade,
Papá planed leftover lumber, groomed the grain
With emery rags, nipped shards, buffed to suede
Every nick and scratch then smeared an oily stain;
Armoire, cupboard, credenza, or stool, each made
To outlast mold's caprice, rot's relentless reign—
A cement shed, pawnshop tools, Papá got paid
With cardboard IOU's but didn't complain,
Dallied bills, snubbed calls, worried about dirt
Spoiling beeswax, a runny varnish, the hair
That strayed into seamless shellac, while I gave
Succor to fractures, restored scraps, healed the wart
On a lacquered pine leg, vigilant in my care
Of salvaged wood as it bucked the austere lathe.

Zafra

Province of Matanzas, Cuba, 1919

Season of sugar harvests, saint's day sweethearts:
One-legged François trundles on a donkey cart
Across the rutted roads of mill towns to shoot
Plump brides in starched flax, silk sashes, calfskin boots,
Whose gaunt fathers would plow granite to pay
Dowries, trousseaus, sacristy fees. Night and day
Steam trains freight hogshead molasses, crates of rum,
Sugar gems, at first dirty and blotched, then spun
First water for traders in London, Vienna, Brussels.
Though Europe's in ruins, sharecroppers shuffle
To maracas, three-string guitars, drink the green
Cane juice, the price of sugar highest it's ever been,
Till the market steepens, saturates, succumbs
To traders' glut and soon free-falls like Icarus.

But on this feast of St. Jude, boys romp in the cane
Fields, torching hives of weed, laying down ratsbane,
Slingshooting buzzards that linger for carrion,
While sisters betrothed at twelve fumble rumpled gowns
And primp with cascarilla, coal dust, marrow grease,
Twirl crooked parasols, furl moth-eaten fans as they wheeze
In corsets to pose on rawhide, a screen of cheesecloth.
Most girls would have flirted with the hooded box,
But Grandma Cuca—gelder, cane cutter, roughrider—
Scowls, squirms, silt of makeup cracking, who'd spur
Broncos bareback than sit sidesaddle in the sun.
Wedding bells peal, her eyes sting, throat burns. "Nun
Or whore," she thinks, "you're still a branded mare,"
And seethes with bone satin cinched to a snare.

THOMAS O'GRADY

Exile

Sometimes, exile makes the heart
grow harder than the iron edge,
exposed at last, of a long-discarded
cartwheel in the sand. The calloused
sole of absence, distance dulls
all but the phantom pain of taking
leave until I walk this stony
foreign shore.

At home the russet strand gives way
beneath soft feet except
where knuckly knots of mussels
barnacle themselves to salt-brushed
shelves of shale. Encrusted
so, not hardened to the core,
I suffer once more that surging bone-
deep hurt of parting. *At home.* . . .
Washed by that tide, my brittle bedrock
heart erodes.

Lament for My Family, Lost at Sea

So small that rain-besotted, wind-plagued place—
so shipwreck-shallow its surrounding seas.
Unmoored at last, cast off with derelict
concern, we swore to plant our masts—each sail
trimmed to a blazoned flag saluting *Life!*—
atop some lofty point of no return.

The thrill of risking all for a rich return—
hedging our bets, wagering that win, place
or show, we could find ourselves set for life:
how brazenly we held to that half-seas
over hope of catching fortune in full sail—
the blind-drunk dream of every derelict.

Already in our minds that derelict
coast, high and dry against the tide's return,
filled the horizon bright as a mainsail
spread before the four winds' will. Why not place
our trust in the billowing seven seas?
The way the delve and churn of Island life

dragged incessantly on, long as a life
sentence, who would dare judge us derelict
for choosing transportation overseas?
Guilt-free—knowing no jury could return
a verdict just to put us in our place—
with such giddy innocence we set sail.

Or ignorance. To watch those stormclouds sail
overhead dark as Fate yet for the life
of us never think twice that we might place
ourselves in peril—O such derelict
common sense! But how we spurned the return
of native wisdom, taking to the Seas

of Faith and Doubt like stars in a high-seas
drama of our own plotting, as if sail
and spar were actors' props we might return
to backstage storage, and our plight—true life-
and-death—was less real than that derelict
schooner ablaze in legends of the place.

Now how these heartless seas batter sheer life—
the salt-tattered sail of our derelict
souls. O to return to that harboring place. . . .

War Stories

An old soldier, my father's father,
survived the Kaiser's cruel juggernaut

(what were the odds?) to tell the tale
of how his regiment, the King's Liverpool,

decimated—the dead beyond all counting—
his good fate led him behind the lines

to a kindred band: farmboys, fishermen,
P.E.Islanders—helping, allied hands.

What were the odds that one of that small
company (his name now worn away by fame-

defacing time) had boarded the war-bound train
at Bear River station on the sort of morning

dogs love—especially a pup called Rowdy
who lives on still in local lore? The story

goes that each afternoon that forlorn mutt returned
to await his master by the disappearing tracks—

until the day the bad news came by singing wire
that another brave youth had fallen before that

rolling engine of death. *What were the odds?*
What canine sense foreknew the end

that no ordinary soul, and least of all
the railroad agent (my mother's father—

what were the odds?) uncoding that sad message,
indelible dot by dash, would dare to portend?

O what were the odds that fourscore years later,
I would page through his Telegrapher's guide

for some hint of how he bore up under
that burden of darkening doorways, grim cablegram

in his grip, and wonder if each casualty
left him as literally lost for words as I when

I heard of my boyhood friend—his mournful parents,
his wife, his dog—and could find only FULL STOP.

Thanksgiving

Summers we'd give thanks to be city born
and bred when, come mid-August, our country
cousins trudged two weeks ahead to the stern
task of learning, the clean-cut drudgery
of school. Of course, in October we'd curse
the luck that gave them a fortnight repeal
of break-knuckle rules—though what could be worse
than digging potatoes in muck-caked fields?
Who, in their right minds, would envy that chore,
and pray—in late November, a thousand
miles and many years away—to restore
themselves by the grace of clay-coated hands?
Elbow-deep in a sack of unscrubbed spuds,
we swear never to wash off that red mud.

Epithalamia

1. "They Became Mermaids"

The wet centre is bottomless.

Local legend has it how, beleaguered
by a frothing mob of pent-up gallants—
brothers, uncles, cousins, all with talents
of a cutthroat sort, a bold *avant-garde*
hard bent on making right a sordid wrong—
a sorcerer asked his abducted bride
would she take the plunge. How could she decide?
To which dark camp would she rather belong?
The story goes that the cold wizard swept
her into the lake's unfathomable heart,
down a churning channel drawn on no chart,
out to the open sea. I think she leapt.
Tales tell of a seal-like pair basking bare
on the rocks: sometimes they come up for air.

2. A Bicycle Built for Two

Learning (they say) is a light burden; from
what little I've learned over time, marriage
too may be borne like any other sum
or substance worth its own weight. By carriage,
trundle cart, or barrow we transport goods
to here and there; by wagon, truck or train—
bridging rivers, traversing tangled woods
by elevated track or rutted lane—
freight rolls along, no more cumbersome a load
than what that couple on that bright tandem
in the song distributed as they rode:
life's cargo squared, not conveyed at random.
Love (I've learned) is an axle made of steel:
every morning reinvent your wheel.

3. The Fixed Link

Never build a marriage like a nine-mile bridge—
engineering pre-fabricated parts,
trusting trestled feet sunk by a delving dredge
(drafted first to scale on blueprinted charts)
can truly withstand the stress of ice-packed
seas and the mass of a steel-girded bed
on top. God knows how time and tide exact
their tax and toll on whatever sits dead
in the water—how all that will endure
sails free of conformity and fixed notions,
like that rigged-out schooner ablaze offshore
in local lore: a phantom of the oceans.
Make marriage burn like a ship spurning land:
weigh anchor, link by link, hand over hand.

JOHN PHILLIP SANTOS

Piedras Negras

Seventeen days in Mexico comes down to coins
in my pocket. Pesos, three nickels
I find a dime in my wallet.
Up to a mile away, beggars hear the clink of coins
and I'm ringing mine openly.
They will come dressed in their parents' clothes
and uncle's hat; they'll look at the lines of my palms
when they take my lode of coins.
Alone at the edge of the country
all my souvenirs, the memory of having been somewhere
mingle and settle like a dust
across the back of my shoulders.
Every time the wind rises up
I lose a bit of what's happened.
Consider my cargo; a clay flute, bought for eighty pesos,
the wool blanket, a pauper's bargain at two hundred,
the day I traded six ball-point pens for a pair of sandals.
And there were beggars everywhere
Asking for money, a vegetable for their morsel stews
or just money. Some sat on church steps
giving out pictures of saints in return for tiny change.
They appeared in my dreams as deer, donkeys, and goats
that I would feed all day and night.
Before you leave a place behind you,
give everything to the beggars,
come away weightless, take your shoes off at the door.

Today the beggars do not arrive.
across the street, a boy in a wolf-mask
yells that he is going to eat me. Some women walk by
with bundles of wet alfalfa on their backs.
Looking for beggars in Mexico, nothing is as big
as a fifty-cent piece, ordinary people the size
of Emiliano Zapata's eyes
going white in all the old photographs.

The Fredericksburg Screen

Veni Redemptor, but not in our time,
Christus Resurgens, quite out of this world.
'Ave' we cry; the echoes are returned.
Amor Carnalis is our dwelling-place.
> —Geoffrey Hill, *Tenebrae*

Cedars stooped to sweep near my dwelling.
Rain clouds clustered there, then moved South.
In this way, the wind kept things going.
Two winds headed gulfward, dust and rubbish
with them, arching the trees back to themselves,
leaving them hunched down or kneeled at the shore.
There, the mighty trunks lean over, pointing
out, on the expanding face of the Gulf.
Then live oaks lined up like a field of priests.
Animals stirred there, leaping from the branches.
Aphids, bores, and caterpillars made meals
on the bark. Wind looked out in all quarters.
At the cliffs past Fusco's, echoes sputtered
and disappeared at last in the canyon.
On a donkey, I made my way against the wall
arriving then at the bottom. The rubble
of twenty years was there—kitchenette chairs,
lumber of old houses, something gold in a lump of shit.
Something tumbled into a pile of rusty tin.
Leaves were falling from above, over the bluffs
down to me, on the floor, where old newspapers
celebrated the centennial of this town's founding.
Banners had flown out over the streets of Fredericksburg,
new flowers were scattered through the cemetery,
a live deer was chained to a parking meter,
a day illuminated by the past, and the mayor

in the omni-congregational church retold
his story of the settlement. The floods had come,
then returned after the sickness, and then the fire,
and I found old Fenmore, leading his mule
back from town. He was almost Mexican
when Mexicans were not allowed to stay.
And many would die, they said, drowning in a creek
or falling asleep in front of an advancing train.
That day we rode to the empty stables
with his pictures of the Virgin of Guadalupe.
Fenmore remembered the tornado that took his wife.
He'd broken horses for a living, so his bones were bent.

———

It began for me earlier with the cattle, when
they would await us in their pastures by the road
to Fredericksburg: The Santa Gertrudis, the Brahma,
Herefords, and Angus—they were the great breed,
stupid and enormous, masticating their elegant cud
with a steady twine of drool swooning from their lips.
I gave a black cow the holy name *Asunción*.
Then I found a cow dead, struck by lightning.
Of my talking to cows there is not much to be said,
only that we could line up alongside a fence
and sing low *moooo*-cow, and then they'd come,
to stare, or stick their bobbing heads over the wire.
What preserved them was their utter lack of imagination.
There was no need to go anywhere, the rain
came upon them and left their hides refreshed, the sun
and moon exchanged quarters, the open pastures
bristled with new grass. That was the mercy of the world.
And we'd drop the blocks of salt from the first field
out all the way to the cow's pond, chopped cactus
or burned yucca for fodder when the pasture was low.

Then they fought among themselves, the bite marks
of a bull or flesh grazed on the fence's barbs.
In the night, from the shack, we heard horns lock,
their great lungs abounded, thundering around us.
Adolf died, left his cattle without a father, so we kept
the place until Merrill could take it over himself,
and that summer was a hot one, the tongues hung down
from the heavy jaws, the muddle of manure turned
quickly into dust, what finally would remain, we supposed,
would remain. And we expected only that the Pedernales
could continue flowing and something in the ground
would suggest that the pines might throw their cones,
for in this way things could be kept going.
But Merrill let the thing fall, fences fell, wind
fell hard onto the house and slammed the shutter,
and hooves-up, the cows perished in the empty pastures.
We dragged their carcasses from the back of the old truck,
In that land on end, in our tumbled down world.

Epistle on History

~ *to Adam Ashforth, at Finstock*

No dialogue should include a tiddly-wink mood,
my fever beneath this tea-colored light, or the way
the clouds rattled and blew today, when you took
your spokes and chains and dawdled back for Oxford,
but all things coming apart, Compadre: the world's
a ragged rickshaw, not a ruby on a turtle's back.
The fire which men once worshiped is crept into
every chimney, burning rubble, or newspapers, or time.
That dandelion, a fair plant, and tall; see
the deceptive way it's rearranged with the day's passing?
A flowering first, then a kind of sphere made of knobs?
What moves the thing, if not will? Chemistry,
perhaps, memory without intellect,
or maybe some latitude that's scrawled right in the dirt.
Mendel knew nothing of peas or plants like these.
The wind caterwauls across the hedge roots
and plucks the seeds like the last hairs
from old Dolly's pate. Thus creation
first kisses the forehead of sure annihilation,
the way Spenser saw it in his *Preludium*
to Book Five of *The Faerie Queene*,
or Donne, in his *Anniversaries*, the gloomy chant:
Shee, shee is dead; shee's dead: when thou knowst this,
Thou knowst haw wan a Ghost this our world is. . . .
and then again, Shiva makes his toothy shuffle
on the fried pall of what we've loved in this world.
Yet it's too delicious to be true, isn't it?
The theme of decline that's not without purpose?
It's fit for embroidery, or a plodding Sabbath sermon.
What's real is this blank space, that rises in our bread
or belches up from the gut. It's the mirror trick
we all have to play by, dreaming or awake.

I saw your Mother pick a primrose, and braid it
with her past. What fell away was the darkness
like dew rilling from the stem, but this
at best is delusion, and the very best we can know.
And then I will imagine a pleiad of Negroes,
black mussel-eaters, Hottentots,
and how they welcomed the flags of the Dutchmen,
smiling on some beach in sixteen twenty-three.
Or the Aztecs, my own, and their limbs spangled
with feathers. Cortes saw power in their strangeness.
He made them feed on rocks and reeds and scree.
This is the frequency of the vanquished, a kind of death
that loses its spindle as it gets farther from
some sympathy for itself. So the Mexicans
worship horses now, and like Arabs, the black men
wander the world. You wander out now Adam,
and bevel some idea of this shifting plenum
into iron, glass, limestone, or tin.
Your friend will count again the lights you've
seen before, across the hill, at Charlbury.

La Diosa de Maguey

The huisaches were alive with monarchs
and chapote bushes bristled with galaxies of ants.
Thorny garrabatos, like the claws of a cat,
trailed spiderwebs, as banners in her honor.

In this desert flamenco heaven, I wondered
if the skin of her neck tasted of leche quemada,
if her breath had the fragrance of flowery yolixpi.

But she sat alone, draped in a fiery serape,
singing to tecolotes as they floated past her on the hilltop.

"Es la sirena de la sierra," the old vaquero called her.
"Do not dance with that demonia colorada!"

She made the sky turn the color of maguey,
a phosphorus greenish grey, and in that baptismal light,
her flesh glowed with a thousand ghostly thorns.

I would set myself before her, if she allows me
avoiding her eyes behind the undulating veils,
and leave behind my offerings:
exquisite sierra honey, an apple dipped in chile,
a green and pink grasshopper, encased in fresh beeswax.

MICHAEL SMITH

Anagrammatic Ode to Emily Dickinson

I.

I too run sick of silences, still language,
        long take of shadow
seen on both house and bush, sun's maze
        (heat, arc, dip, and age)—tender eye
yoked to the ease of home.

Given: a poem is always confession,
        the mete end always tease,

a concession. (I am more
than this I bleed.)

Entered, the world is a jail (isn't it?)
        hooded, small. Beaten,

we burrow.

II.

Arrest of the heroic: to sap that hue
or thrust (ha) in the sounds of the quick . . .

You strived to tell them
(but handed the moment, the world posed)

then threw them fewer, your meteors,
tender dots tethered (my term,

my error) to the jutted edge of day

(Oh, your glint I envy most . . .)

The wisdom is simple, but varied.

It's won by reaching down.

*The body of the poem is an anagram of Emily Dickinson's poems # 241,
441, and 475 insofar as all of the letters of the three Dickinson poems
have been used (once and only once) in the formation of this poem. No
letters have been added and no letters have been left out.*

Small Industry

Franklin, Swimming

Out back the grapes are overripe and falling.
It's colder here already. Wind from the north
follows the river where I walk to find
in the concrete and iron of a dead industry
water is caught, funneled and shot to no
purpose now, though once a year the sportsmen come
and there's a fair.
        (More than miles and centuries, I think,
separate us tonight.)
        Industry. Beside a pool, I stand
(as years ago he and I would sometimes stand) and watch
water still lap the banks where the impulse died
or moved away, and tonight, I think of you,
but as a boy, before your father's prose
claimed its swift and clear victory.

For years the story stuck with me.
Not the sane and reasonable plan you made of it
years later, but as it must have been: wading in,
then on a whim retrieving your kite
and under the wind's power, crossing
the mile-wide lake; how with the thought, the bright face
must have brightened, watching the kite as it rose
or suddenly swerved with greater purpose;
how as you neared the center, when you reached
where you believed the true center of the lake
must be, your knuckles stiffened and whitened,
eyes following the thin, glistening line
until they were blinded by a kite no longer
a kite, but a sun; and how, when you could, you opened

your eyes to see, on the other side, your friend,
the footnote, your clothes under his arm, patient,
waiting his turn, though puffed and flushing where he stood . . .

I. Apostrophe to Philippi

Miles pass, and mountains, and rounding a curve
I think I know, I am (for the first time in 20 years)
snatched back to see, O Philippi, you,
spread out in all your splendor before me.

A trollop without panties, or so once my mother wrote
(a poet, too, and angry), having in mind
your mines, but also the leggy way
the one road in and out of your valley
softly angles at your center.

Philippi, she didn't do you justice . . .

Your river now is low, but I remember
when the water rose to split
you down the middle, how it steeped
so high in its swell your streets,
he had to row us out in a boat.

Splendor! You are
this river and Civil-War-circa covered bridge . . .
train tracks, courthouse, museum and church,
three bars, an A&P, plus
assorted small houses (one
in particular) and, if you count it,
a college atop the highest mountain.

Little town, you
unsettle me.

It's been awhile, I know, but I'm still your son, still
his son, and, as such, I say (un)to you:

Stay small, Philippi,
Hunker down, Philippi,

for even now I fear he must be getting on
(he who flashes through my mind,
flushed with wine and all action).

Philippi, this wasn't meant to be a history,
but can it be that nothing's changed?
Am I again your rowdy boy?

North, on business, I turned your way
only when I saw the sign.
No crisis summoned me.
He's still alive, with a wife, and a house
half way up one of your smaller mountains,
finally safe from your floods.

Philippi, I have no answer for this endeavor.
Am I here to take or to retrieve?

You are not needed, but do you need?

II.

He picked me up from mother's in his truck
and on the clock. I tuned the radio
as he filled me in
on the job we headed for. Then we were there.

I remember the mud-clumped yard, the Ford
wheel-less under the tarp, a door opening
and a hand beckoning.
Drawing back from the heater's brownish smell,

I was careful not to knock the water pot
from the top and ignored the diapered child,
thin, running wild
under the woman's frown,

as he began, then straightened and softly
explained he'd ordered the wrong blessed part.
He sort of shrugged
as she began her curses,

following us into the yard and past
the Ford. But mostly I remember his face,
not the faintest trace
in his cheeks of anger or pride, he stood

and simply nodded by the truck, hand fast
on the latch, eyes twice darting to catch my eyes,
not in search of understanding,
just to see where I was looking.

III.

Down 77 to 40 by way of 52.
North Carolina: to be near her father's family;
Greensboro: because she liked the schools.

(Already, it seems, I'd turned my back on prose.)

Those first months she worked two jobs:
English teacher at Southeast High,
and, evenings, hostess at a local restaurant.

From our window I watched the nighttime cars go by,

and so in class remained a step behind.
The accent deemed problematic, but correctable,
for years they tried to draw it out of me.
Cold fingers squeezed my *h'it* into an *it*
but left a funny taste in my mouth.

(What's more at odds than an urban South?)

As for him?
                        No word
until Christmas,

and no one home but me to take the call.
I told him: no snow, just heavy frosts.
But hail one time the size of his fists.

IV.

Village within a village, town
within the town. Gall Street, then Boyle
and Sycamore, which follows the river.
(and all the houses there twins of one another)
Your mines shut down and your theater gone,
and everyone scrambled to Clarksburg, Elkins.

Perpetual flame and a fog that never lifts . . .

But from the start he preferred a solo act:
any rima to renga: knife seller, repairman,
hummingbird. Take the day he stripped, then
(as from the bank we watched) performed
across and back every textbook stroke.
A good distance even in that summer of drought,
so surely he was not the unflappable comfort
of my recollection, the ripples rising
and breaking before the cresting, quivering chin.

For our part—
        Yard sales, and, once, a magic show
(the table listing on my crouched brother's back);
Coke bottles rinsed and taken to Mark at the Red Star
(until the night he shot himself, or was shot,
then it was Luke we brought them to);
a weekly walk up the mountain to Nan and Pop's;
occasional thefts.
        —This isn't the poem I thought I'd write,
I confess, but easing the rental to the curb,
I find the old house well, and almost
as I pictured it.

V. Aqua Velva

For just one whiff tonight I'd swipe, I swear, a case of it.
If I could find the stuff these days.

Of the three, one trip down from the mountain I remember.
Or is it I remember the three trips as one?

Crossing the bridge he once helped save, passing
the house we'd all given up on almost a year ago,

we found his place, two rooms
above Tim's Hardware and Small Engine Repair, plus

a tar-covered balcony overlooking the river.
(She honked twice and dropped me with a kiss at the stairs.)

How could I forget dinner outside at the Big T's?
And later, my head against his shoulder, I let myself breathe deeper

as moonlight through the window bathed our faces blue.
Or was it the television screen, left on for my sake, blue

and flickering?

VI.

Village within a village, town
within the town. Sycamore, Boyle Street and Gall.
Philippi, even your mountains lack the jag
of holiday, and nothing surfs the streams
that wind their way from cap to river
like an author reading his own books.

(Perpetual flame and a fog that never lifts . . .)

A Sunday, and in my mind no memory of sound
beyond the scrape of his boot against the door
as we moved to join the resolute cold
of December, his heavy step
forcing the crust of snow to expose
its mantle of mud below. As always,
only the tracks remained uncovered.

A Sunday, and after halftime he couldn't stand
to watch, so as Bradshaw and the Steelers played
toward a record fourth, he sent us down and out,
or waved us long, past the tipple.
(We counted ties and prayed our grip would hold.)
When his bottle gave out, he spun it
so it pointed north along the rail,
toward Pittsburgh, and the trains,
and the coal that fed the fires that formed the steel.

ANTHONY WALTON

Third Shift

Mickey says hey
you guys, go throw
eleven, which means
for me and Knox to unstack
and stack a hundred
hundred pound sacks
of corn starch or dextrose,
or whatever,
off a truck out of St. Louis
or Decatur or Kansas City.
Midnight, and we will be
loading and unloading
until dawn.
Next it might be barrels
of animal fat bound
for Memphis, or sifted grain
destined to become cereal
for the breakfasts
of the middle west.
We don't know
or care, we just throw it,
get out of the way,

and stand on the dock
taking deep breaths and waving
the next guy in.
Then maybe it's break,
Knox and me on the roof,
him smoking and singing
about some woman or another
and making bad jokes about misery

loving company. I smile,
and because he knows
it will make me laugh,
he sings "Since I Fell For You"
off-key and with the wrong
words, and I look out over
the highway toward Iowa,
wondering which headlights
are headed here. Then I take
a hit, and it's time to go back.
It's always time to go back.
I am thinking of a night
when I was younger and didn't know
that life could be like this,
how I took Amtrak out of South
Bend, coming home to bury
my best friend. In Chicago
the train stopped behind a mill
on 35th Street
and I could see a man sweating
and stoking a blast furnace.
It was August, the sky going
orange to pink, and it looked
like he was working the gates
of hell. I am learning to think
of these gates as such, because
it's hotter than hell,
Mickey is cursing the day
he was born, Knox is singing
about misery, which is its own
company, and two more trucks
are backing in, steady
as the gravity dragging us
into the ground.

Elegy for Joan (1955–1986)

You did not bend
or break,
but simply sailed
away.

I could only chase as your heavy blossom snapped
and snagged in the wind,
over waves of grass, trees, flowers . . .

Too soon. The epistle of my grief lengthens
each night, I revise
but cannot send.

I can spend my days anywhere, Times Square,
in a field of faces
                    running for the train
or back in Illinois considering
a field of infinite blue cornflowers,
but having outlived your death, I can't outlive
you. Time passes,
                    but what is time
except the never-ending present punctuated
by what it takes away?

You knew you were dying
and you did
            with an equanimity so full of peace
it bordered on rage, which is where
I live
        and owe you goodbye.

Not this mooning through cities,
through blue fields holding your face
like a flower before me, my blossom
in bloom,
        already doomed.

Insomnia

4 A.M., reading Mandelstam,
the brittle cries of sparrows
punctuating the efficient music
made by trashmen making their way
up the street, making a living.

The sharp moon remains
a wound in the sky, the quiet stars
my congregation, waiting for daylight
to walk on in like a nightwatchman,
whistling through darkness.

A trash can bangs
and I think of Mandelstam,
conscript in the army of the dead,
disappearing like a scrap of paper blown
downwind, whispering *I will rise again*
to say the sun is shining . . .

If the day is a flare marking the dark road,
the soul is a candle,
fanning over the horizon, nodding
and refusing sleep.

McDonald's, Scottsboro, April, 1997

The white girl smiles
and hands me
my meal, perfectly
happy, it seems,
to see me, a black

man smiling
and accepting
a warmed-over
quarter-pound of meat
with cheese.

I am on the road,
rolling through
Jackson County,
here for food and gas
on my way
to Tennessee.

The way her pink
and silver-ringed
fingers touch mine—
so benign, as if time
and the town were
as innocent as she.

What is this to me,
who needs to eat
and keep moving,
to be in Tennessee
by midnight? I resolve
to leave history

behind me, resuming
my journey, the ride
up U.S. 72 into
and through Jackson
County, into what I fear
and only remember,
and only remember here

Gwendolyn Brooks

Sometimes I see in my mind's eye a four or five
year old boy, coatless and wandering
a windblown and vacant lot or street
on the windblown South Side. He disappears
but stays with me, staring and pronouncing
me guilty of an indifference more callous
than neglect, condescension as self-pity.

Then I see him again, at ten or fifteen, on the corner,
say, 47th and Martin Luther King, or in a group
of men surrounding a burning barrel off Lawndale,
everything surrounding vacant or for sale.
Sometimes I trace him on the train to Joliet
or Menard, such towns quickly becoming native
ground to these boys who seem to be nobody's
sons, these boys who are so hard to love, so hard
to see, except as case studies.

Poverty, pain, shame, one and a half million
dreams deemed fit only for the most internal
of exiles. That four-year-old wandering
the wind tunnels of Robert Taylor, of Cabrini
Green, wind chill of an as yet unplumbed degree—
a young boy she did not have to know to love.

HENRY WEINFIELD

from *Sonnets Elegiac and Satirical*

Two

The park was where we found ourselves alone,
As if it always had been there for us
In some dimension where the sun shone
And we were naked and anonymous.
It was as if it always had been thus,
And always would be there for us to feel,
As if each moment were continuous—
And so it seemed, although it wasn't real.
It was the loveliest day of many a year,
The loveliest day of this dark century,
Almost too beautiful for us to fear
That we were taken in adultery.
The sun eclipsed the world, and it was dark;
And yet it shone for us that day inside the park.

Three

Plato's Republic was no place for us—
We had no business in that perfect state;
For there the poet, deemed superfluous,
Was not admitted through the iron gate.
Republics must be kept inviolate
From those who hunger for the Beautiful:
You are too beautiful to contemplate,
And I am no philosopher at all.
The Golden Age could not be found in Greece
Without a detour through the land of truth:
Plato's Republic postulates police
To curb the anarchic power of sexual youth.
The borderguards have warned us, and we know
That we must leave, but have no place to go.

Six

Heroic love, which yearns to be unique,
Despite the common mould in which it's cast,
Concocts a magic potion, so to speak,
To purge the future of its burdened past.
We know, of course we know, that what we taste
Is either fatal or ephemeral;
We know that nothing can be made to last,
That nothing lasts if it is beautiful.
What lasts is nothing, then; what lasts is death—
Death is where heroes make their last abode;
Death is the poison which gives love the faith,
With its last breath, to sing the *Liebestod*.
Embracing death, convinced that we are gods,
We sing forever—against all the odds.

Seven

The early Christians were so confident
That they could reconcile opposing views,
They turned the lamp that lit the Occident
Upon the darker wisdom of the Jews.
Their concept was that God could interfuse
The entire universe with His sole plan;
Omniscient and omnipotent, could choose
Miraculously to become a man.
But men are murderers, and all their art
The skin-stretched lampshade of idolatry.
—This bitter knowledge set the Jews apart
Through all their wanderings through history:
Their God was imageless; He had no name;
And though they prayed to Him, He never came.

An Essay on Violence

"But words of reason drop into the void . . ."
Simone Weil,
The Iliad; or, the Poem of Force

Who would have thought that what the sages taught
With such devotion would have gone for naught,
Forgotten in the coils of violence?

Who would have thought that it was all in vain,
That what was wrought would be torn down again,
That nothing would remain but violence?

Who in those distant ages would have thought
That repetition would be still our lot
And echoing laments of violence?

But words of reason drop into the void
And perish there, by violence destroyed,
In ever-widening pools of violence.

We are the playthings of that history,
The instruments of its dominion, we,
And gross materials of violence.

Subjects, we are subjected to the powers
Which have their being in not being ours,
And which we summon up in violence.

System gives way to system, class to class;
Mere transient forms, to nothingness they pass,
Suborning and suborned by violence.

Marx thought that with the bourgeoisie destroyed
True harmony at last would be enjoyed:
The consequence was merely violence.

Christ's admonition, "Turn the other cheek,"
Wrote Nietzsche, is the counsel of the weak:
Must we be martyrs, then, to violence?

And yet we know that to respond in kind
Is to succumb to forces that are blind
And cut both ways—the powers of violence.

Suffering, wrote Sophocles, can drive us mad;
Madness deprives us of what sight we had,
Conferring blessings upon violence.

Jihads, crusades . . . with labels such as these
We demonize our foes and thus appease
With sacrifice the gods of violence.

Whoever acts in concert with God's will
May abrogate His stricture not to kill:
It is not killing then or violence.

Whoever is the messenger of God
Need not forbear to shed a little blood:
The greater good requires violence.

"The highest wisdom and the primal love,"
Wrote Dante, are the attributes that drove
Our Maker to make Hell's eternal violence.

I beg to differ with the Florentine:
Your violence is yours and mine is mine.
It was not God conceived of violence.

God, if He but existed, would be good!
Would rid the world of evil, if He could,
The imagination of its violence.

He and His utmost seraphim on high
Are utterly unable, though they try,
To solve the antinomies of violence.

We are the ones from whom that seed is sown
And have to bear its burden on our own
And all alone face up to violence.

Read in these repetitions the lament
Reverberating through past ages spent
That we should do or suffer violence.

Song for the In-Itself and For-Itself

The in-itself and for-itself
Were two dimensions of the self.
The in-itself was satisfied
With any crust that fed its pride,
Hinging a self upon the pelf
Which it had smuggled to itself.

The for-itself, its opposite,
Burned with desires infinite;
Nor could it ever find repose,
Allow the boundaries to close
On any possibility.
Preferring anonymity,
It stared into a boundless gulf,
Forever searching for itself.

Like any Ghibelline or Guelf,
The in-itself arranged a self
In some proposed delineation—
A name, identity, or nation,
Accommodating to itself
The views of every other elf.

Meanwhile its counterpart knew all
The aphorisms of Pascal
By heart, and would reflect upon
Our penchant for delusion;
Our infinite capacity
For falsehood and duplicity;
Our vanity, profanity,
Habitual inhumanity;
How all our projects always tend
To come to nothing in the end,
Since what we are is more or less
Projected out of nothingness.
And so on and in similar vein
The for-itself would thus complain,
Abusing mankind for his folly
In litanies of melancholy.
But when the for-itself would rant,
Thinking itself still dominant,
The in-itself would softly creep
Into its bosom, lull it to sleep—
Until at length its griefs being told
The inconsolable was consoled
And a new cycle thus begun,
Though nothing new beneath the sun.

The in-itself and for-itself
Were two dimensions of the self.
This couplet chorus-like rehearses
The initial premise of these verses.
The self was bitterly divided
And each the other part derided,
With no abatement of their strife
Ensuing while they took in life—
And hence no way of putting closure
Upon our poems paltry measure.
Enough! We'll leave them on the shelf,
The in-itself and for-itself.

JOHN WILKINSON

Facing Port Talbot

1

What little mutes within our mouldy covers, has weight,
drew devotee manikins would scrunch through cracker stars

inflate a life-saving ring, their sacs were frictionless,
were sterile with the buoyancy of a head start, itinerary

wired to upstage their processors' conveyor facelift—
pressure for renewal, lightsome at their spread wings

would shut the hatch, taught on each approach they flicker
never touching, who else's natural chaos billows free

above a hard-bitten surface, abstrusing out in a sphere
of No disturbance; theirs alone the fires supported wicker

harmlessly, unmeasured on those scales the breath skews.
Turn over, bed down, hollow. Keep your head down under

laths of heavenly light, hair-schemes of forgetfulness,
pull the impetiginous stars. When occupying a point of fact

as of arrival, thick with air-borne motes, make your tally,
chock-a-block with a fly's generations, a checkerboard

droops for the dark to match, blinding a spot in radiance,—
turn right over, into the small of the back dark & hollow

showing no score, but neither of these but dense alloy—
intact should we set about us, swing, saturate this gauze

stiff already with fleas, crumbs & sweat, ensconce a view
well underneath, may it muffle the crash of percussion

introduced the first few bars, shall we congeal a universe
would sufflate. What's left behind, steams energetically

on a flat stone cannot take the heat, undulates as tide
marks the shoreline with its skinfull of protected figures

held on station as corresponding dream levels subside.
This was some shadow's fidelity. Heavens above, for piles

of atmosphere smelt down, drawn off them a brute or angel
threads the coast whose contours, marker buoys & nets

entangle loosely, the cone of a gated creature's sustaining
locks each in its open weave, a heaven's gate of mockery.

The flag shall start the loop. Foundering through stars
unclock time, & eternity is that ring of harshest light

besets the enlightened, all space has been brought to task
in a single expression, personal as it flows back & round.

2

The long & short of it & the first & last, meet & have
the foresight to cope; these like not the drops commingle,

slide without a trace into circulation, but true tears
dwell in the cusp of splitting the difference, soak the

cover here & now, there-there, your place or mine. How
contrary as pans held in balance! A topgallant stargleams,

swings like a pair of lovers dash their creatures of rag
Matted through the disloyalty of the substyle, shadowless,

we dig the pit, the trench which burdens with slow oil
a wick capillaries, thickening with smoke a slight barrow.

3

Hush your face. Under rubbish-dumps where carrion feed
tangy in their basin, this sound we'd never heard before

much-travels, but comes back to slope, to the inseparables:
according to their lights. By theirs, who work audiences

collectively recursive in their need to fail faithfully,
queue at the door for refunds, they leave hand-in-hand,

say goodnight which means good-morning as the broken doll
reassembles in their great recovery of fellow-feeling.

Mattresses still smoulder like the depths of slept hay
are burnt by urine; loving voices have been packed & steam

an eye for an eye, put one over, fortunate, I'd swear this,
wincing dead theatrically. Skin absorbs to parry or defeat

a main thrust, but detail does not suffer—once we join,
though great revenge threatens, hairline cracks still provide:

Ransacking for meat & potatoes busying the savannah,
crossed with bells swung rickety on stanchions, at raises

gather the rucks; do their squeals blurt from wounds on a
testing bed, a white pit they crawl out of? Four sockets

but five exit-wounds spread, terrifically the sea rears,
tail-enders knuckle their shaggy heads, then stand upright.

Some were easily adept, switched from heel to ball as
though ice worked beneath, balance & sway neatly relaxed

Get packing their own share in polystyrene caskets. Hear
this while they live: it will agitate & put skates under

patricide like green shoots, the auditor-as-Nimrod draws
a bead across ice. At the blow-hole a cascade of bells,

allure the wax penis stitched between wandering lights
dives for & near-misses, mountains quake, breakers crumple

Quiet domestic fur leaps out of its skin. News of progress
smokes on the ridge, flares, but listen! in low swells

peaks imperturbable the conch & horn shall hail from
dock for dock, in step function feeding back to retrench.

Tit-for-tat I'd call it, serves them right, even-handedness
distorts the void cavity, the magpies plunging in feel

flummoxed by soft mess, a doll which cries & does wee-wee,
tousles from the deep moist box its own ghosts pilfer.

.

London Fields From Afar

Whether market forces
or upsurge in confidence
　　　picks up their heels,
the drop-shadow slope makes
a grounded look
before the tilting windows.
　　　　Why then scurry
over the fens like crazy hearts
　dressed in sun-
　　　shine or moon-allowance.

Windows open so far.
Misery belts out the sunken vowel
stupid in its pot of
　Now Jump
as legislation or style altogether
state their own state.
　　Jump & land in shadow
breaks their legs
then flounder like clouds stop
over the Amazon.

Watch out for skin texture.
At ground level light goes turbid
on the young thick wheat.
　　Where did the allergen
spray rise,
　　　over no advance?
This is to burn, a spy glass
kindles & will blister
　　to admire or even pluck.

But stay.
       Affluence in a capsule
will trump the next hand.
          Moonshine has less
  going for its fisty shafts,
its spill
      of antic vowels
than the canter of such chains
the sun against the skin is locked into—

phase transition. Dust rises
beside the mauve ledge & marble
      hits liquidity. Striate
over the mineral hills
plumes of vapour
blot down, their lustre
swiped between the legs' withdrawal

or as glamour counts,
but fruits weight & the granaries
shut your gob or gape
       resequenced to be sterile
     shall not, can never detain.
      Run with the refugees
along Mare Street
to London Fields, Elysium:
Ensoulment is an instant's work
    The ears pop
     The eyes water.

Better the Fence

Better the fence
           than the even blink
of green corn with wilderness

Better the fence
           than the squawking
wrist advising the certain cave
"be careful now."

In the compound
we can do much as we like

but in the simple orbit
lorries drain & dribble out,
           yellow suffuses the eye.

Better the fence
           than daisy-ball
stipple that judges your attempt
ahead of you

Better the fence
           than all the frames unbe-
knownst holsters lock open

gluten allergy
alabaster fever,
bales of the humming invisible
           make mutinous its curtate.

Within this shield
we skip as though also-ran

ran to an unrehearsed track
of saturated white

tight as fruit but less penetrable
triggers violently.

Better the fence
        than wild oats, poppies
or ergot that will spoil the crop

Better the fence
        than the pinwheel
disturbances that grind obvious
dark/dazzle lenses

or their interface:
        twist the Etruscan device
against the bank, set it spinning.

Marram Grass

The xerophiles
break down mouths of agitated burrows,
straggle over pine barrens,
                              tongues
loll in a shore-long slurping line-up,
like roughening, like fade,
like smouldering if said of water or like
fluctuating said of opals. Like
filthy mouth, beneath her breath
mutters.
                Combustible
atop a glassed-in wave.
                              Comprehensive
multicolour upload, outputting via red.

Like assertive
        quadbikes & SUVs have carved
salty ducts, power
ribs shuddering to break loose, diesel
trails burn the water
        Shifting of hunched sand
won't deter the xerophiles, self-healing
ramparts were OKed,
        like paths adjust,
voices on the shore drift outward,
        then if scudding home,
speak this margin to a line drawn ragged
further up—
weed or pebbles, buoyant blocks—
blocks carved, blocks erode
into these naiads,
porn stars. The xerophiles trudge past.

Xerophiles throng onto their club floor,
a teeming underthatch,
        soak the wodge of thickener
voluptuous with veins,
                dead sheet, wrinkled verge
sucking at their slow heels,
water strops a salt ledge,
        dogged, automatic, licking
out some lodging place, a lick erosion
                spiriting the sand,
as though pile-up
were a highway's purpose, watch-making
were a whale's, or if a junk oil,
actually it claims here its true flame
stinks & gutters sootily . . .
        look actually the thing was
                the thing was
        saprophyte, delicately lipped
Pan away,
down the coast a new lagoon's cedilla,
isn't
        there the place to gather,
there where stinging whispers clench—
        what else would pine
pickets lodge into,
        plain as day,
        bunch in breathing columns,
converse
like ill wind was said of dust-devils or like
cinematic, said of summer snow.
        Aggrieved & isolated,
stuck on his promontory
a lookout kicks an engine & rips a ditch,

                   the xerophiles'
lips sealed & lids gunged with weeping,
routinely like myelinic sheaths
absorb light's shocks,
reels & cassettes banked against erosion,
            will they mourn prospectively
the micro-habitat in mind, the one
place they ever visit.
Back they stumble
                   xerophiles
dolloped over sand on walkways
concreted with bonds & hot
municipals, their roots
            reputedly provisional, or like
rippling if said of sand wispily or mainly
piled high if said of water.

Statements by the Poets

(A number of the poets in this anthology preferred not to include prose statements. Their poems speak for themselves. —Orlando Menes)

FRANCISCO ARAGÓN

My time as a graduate student at Notre Dame was crucial in two areas where my own work was concerned. My reading of *Rumba Atop the Stones*, coupled with conversations with its author, Orlando Menes, made manifest the notion that a poem can be derived from particular historical events and involve research into those events. This is not a new idea. But I found Menes's "Cuba" analogous to my "Nicaragua"— a country I have yet to set foot in, but which has flourished in my imagination since childhood. And yet, it wasn't until I got to South Bend that I began to write, I think, decent poems that had as backdrop Nicaragua and its history. I still have much to explore in this area, but it began at Notre Dame. The second area of inquiry is companion to the first. I never quite grasped what Thom Gunn meant when he told us undergraduates at UC Berkeley twenty years ago that among the experiences we can mine for our poems is the very act of reading. Twenty years later, John Matthias, like no other teacher before, framed his workshops in such a way that "translation" and "other texts" provided some of the most fertile ground in a writing workshop that I have ever experienced. It may very well be that I was at a point in my writing when I was ready to absorb this lesson, but Matthias illuminated a path that has led me to engage, meaningfully, the texts of Rubén Darío—an ongoing and very personal project.

ROBERT ARCHAMBEAU

When I was an undergraduate in Canada, I was involved with a group of poets devoted to regionalism and the poetry of place, but I was also drawn to Poundian poetry, and all of the European modernism associated with it. I came to Notre Dame to learn from the poet who, I felt, exemplified both the poetry of place and the Poundian tradition better than anyone else: John Matthias. I was fortunate in finding in Matthias a mentor both generous and tremendously erudite, and I benefited tremendously from his tendency to assume the best about the people around him. One of my other professors, Jay Walton, once described this as a kind of inverted egoism on John's part, a personal quirk that caused John to think, "well, if you're in the room with me, you must be interesting!" I learned from many of my professors at Notre Dame, and from my fellow students in the doctoral and M.F.A. programs, but John directed both my M.F.A. thesis and my doctoral dissertation, widening my horizons in the process. In editing a collection of essays on John's work, I sought to pay some small portion of the intellectual and poetic debt I owed him. Notre Dame was good to me in many ways: my first published prose, for example, appeared in the reviews sections of *Religion and Literature* and the then-new *Notre Dame Review*. Although I was happy to escape South Bend for Chicago at the earliest opportunity, I couldn't have asked for a more enlightening and congenial graduate school experience.

KARNI PAL BHATI

I had come to Notre Dame as a graduate student from India in the early 1990s. I thought it an interesting accident that Indiana had an aural and a historical connection with India (rooted in Columbus's original error). Could I also hope to find something here that I didn't know I was looking for? I like to think today that I must have nursed this thought in some form, even then. One of the things I did find was the desire to return to writing poetry, which I had more or less abandoned in pursuit of high theory and criticism in the Ph.D. program. This desire was spurred by my enrollment in a workshop on translating poetry that John Matthias offered one spring term, but it wasn't until Valery Sayers became associate chair of the English department that I mustered the courage to ask if I could be permitted to apply for an M.F.A., as other graduate students before me had done.

My carrel in the Hesburgh library (first on the fourth floor and then on the eleventh) and our married student apartment in the University Village provided just the right space for all my writing. The atmosphere in the University Village, which then had many international student families with children, was such that my wife and children made many lasting friendships while I absented myself to work in my library carrel.

KIMBERLY M. BLAESER

In the long gaze backwards, we can sometimes watch as our accordion soul unfolds, can hear the first sounds of the music we revel in today. The pleasures and possibilities of the writing life began to open for me while I was a graduate student in English at Notre Dame in the 1980s.

Although naive and tentative in both social and literary realms, I enjoyed connections with writers from the Notre Dame community— current *Notre Dame Magazine* editor Kerry Temple, then faculty member Walter Davis, and emeritus professor Ernest Sandeen. I had links with the South Bend creative community through "Writers and Other Troubadours," and each spring, I filled my writer's bellows of curiosity and inspiration as I attended readings, workshops, dinners, and postreading parties held for visiting notables such as Barry Lopez, Robert Pinsky, Ntozake Shange, Seamus Heaney, and Czeslaw Milosz.

In those years of rich discovery, I read widely; not only for classes, but, in the maze of literary crossroads, following the slightest clues— dropped names, epigraphs, allusions, poetic invocations, and bookstore happenstance. With no exposure to practicalities of publication, and long-trained by my reservation background to rein in expectations for my future, I had neither knowledge nor ambition to weigh me down. And so, an exhilaration and sweet satisfaction blew through my writing years at Notre Dame. On a high window ledge off the rear staircase of O'Shaughnessy Hall, the luxurious grounds stretched before me, I might sit with notebook, on a long literary retreat.

JENNY BOULLY

When I was deciding on an M.F.A. program, I kept remembering some advice that a Notre Dame student was given when she was deciding on M.F.A. programs: *get quiet and write*. Notre Dame seemed like a perfect place to get quiet and write. The winters, which began early and stayed late, were so dark and gloomy, that a writer had no choice but to write. I can't say that my first semester at Notre Dame was easy—I took a workshop and a literature course with John Matthias. In addition to writing, John made us read and read a lot. In my first semester, I read almost everything written by Robert Lowell and his contemporaries. I learned about music and prosody. A typical assignment from John went like this: read these chapters in George Steiner's *After Babel*, translate these five poems in three different translation modes as outlined in *After Babel*, compare three different translations of the *Inferno*, and read these articles and this other book. There were times that I thought lightning bolts were shooting out of John, so much did he love poetry and sharing it with his students. He was excited, on fire, and he made us want to reach that kind of excitement. Needless to say, with John and all my wonderful friends and instructors at Notre Dame (and there are so many to list—Valerie Sayers, Steve Tomasula, Sonia Gernes, Gerald Bruns, Stephen Fredman, Orlando Menes, William O'Rourke, to name a few), I learned how to read and write and how to do these things seriously, as if my life depended on it.

JACQUE VAUGHT BROGAN

Of the poems reprinted in this volume, two were written (and published) before I came to Notre Dame (now twenty-three years ago): one when I was a graduate student at the University of Texas, the other when I was an assistant professor (and young mother) at the University of Hawaii. My years at Notre Dame have been marked, personally, by any number of triumphs and losses, a fact which is evident in the "Notes from the Body" series, all written during my time here. But my years at Notre Dame have also been marked by a growing and widening political interest, and with a simultaneous commitment to understanding how our own spirits and The Spirit move and even shape reality in an obviously fractured world. In this regard, my experiences at Notre Dame have proven ever increasingly the old feminist adage that "the personal is political"—a fact which is thoroughly in alignment with Catholicism at its deepest level of commitment. Part Native American myself, I became quite interested and studied what happened with the Potowatami here and with Native Americans elsewhere—a fact which also shows in the poems chosen for this anthology. I would say, in all honesty, that I have grown as a person and as a poet while at Notre Dame—sometimes in spite of it, sometimes because of it.

STACY CARTLEDGE

When I think of my growth as a poet at Notre Dame, one lesson stands out. John Matthias challenged me to write something "of scope." Until this point I had written, as most did, semi-confessional lyrics. The cycle poem that Matthias assigned was a turning point. I wrote "Topography"—which would become my first major publication—an exploration of the interconnections between geography, sanctity, and mathematics. Even the poems collected here, though mainly based in the confessional mode, are not limited to it; at each turn, the poems search out an expansive context into which to fit the details of biography. Notre Dame was a good place to learn this lesson of perspicacity; the grand buildings, the history, and even the name of the school point us towards something bigger than ourselves, a consciousness more than individual, that we should strive for. Only when we reach that far do we approach a truth worth reading.

MICHAEL COFFEY

I came from a very small town in upstate New York. My arrival at the Notre Dame campus in September 1972 provided my first taste of diversity. Even though, by world standards, it wasn't all that diverse, it might as well have been Istanbul to a kid from rural Saranac, New York. What struck me most, however, was the ambition among many of the students, whether academically, athletically, or ethically; and the respect for grace and intellect. I was a newly minted atheist and found myself being mentored, tutored, cajoled, and generally welcomed and even encouraged in my doubt and curiosities by faculty (I had two memorable classes with Father John S. Dunne), administration, and even fellow characters in Fisher Hall. As an adoptee who was raised as an only child by an Irish Catholic family, in an adoption handled by an Irish Catholic foundling home, Notre Dame, in whole, became yet another sheltering and nurturing institution for me, all of which prepared me to look for and find my own shelter and my own nurture, in literature, arts, athletics, and people. Although in retrospect, my callow comportment while an undergrad now seems an insult to these lofty sentiments, a recent and rare return to campus found me weeping at a hallowed spot I had never once before visited: I lit many candles.

JOE FRANCIS DOERR

"Maximus spoke with your tongue: *the thing you're after lies around the bend.*" That is a line from the first significant poem I wrote after arriving in South Bend. It is part of a trio of epistolary poems for three close friends I had left behind in Austin, Texas, friends of whose distance, just three or four short weeks into the fall of 1996, I was already acutely aware. Though my wife Mary and I could not have not have known it at the time, our expectations of spending two years in the frozen north, years that would allow me to pursue an M.F.A. in poetry, were about to be shattered: I was invited to stay on for many more semesters—spring as well as fall—to pursue a Ph.D. in English.

But the real story of my seven-year sojourn at Notre Dame is in, of, and after poetry. I came to Notre Dame after my designs of learning from and working with John Matthias were realized, a realization that has produced a clutch of poems—a few that I wrote, and a few more by others, friends I came to love and admire for themselves and for their words, friends whose distance I now lament. Many of those poems contain a more accurate and appropriate record of time spent at Notre Dame than any careful prose can reconstruct.

KEVIN DUCEY

The place, stuck on the polluted elbow of the St. Joe River, gave us an evocative mix of town and gown. The city gnaws on the memory of Studebaker betrayals, while the university pumps itself up on wonders of legacy; meanwhile down at the ranch, the weekly gun battles between the drive-ups at the Taco Bell vs. the pump-it-yrselfers across the street at the 'Best Italian Beef Sandwich in Town' mini-mart taught us that some things are worth a fresh clip. Classroom discussions could be as fierce. Take it as a sign of a healthy, albeit underground, economy. The money was, and is, hard to spot. John Matthias was my instructor, and through a series of intelligent, provocative readings and assignments, he pushed me to open the field and get what work done as I am able.

BETH ANN FENNELLY

I arrived at the University of Notre Dame in the fall of 1989 thinking I wanted to be an actress. I had just graduated from a very small Catholic all-girl boarding school, and one of the nice things about a small school is that there is so little competition for extracurricular activities. Not only was I in all the school plays, but I usually had the leads—often because no one else was trying out for the role. And my Mom said I was a good actress, so surely I was destined for Broadway, right?

Anyway, when I got to Notre Dame, I tried out for a play, a St. Ed's production. And didn't get the lead. In fact, I didn't get a speaking role. In fact, when the *Notre Dame Observer* reviewed the play, they mentioned the twelve people in the play who did a good job. There were thirteen people in the play. That's how it dawned on me—I was wretched. So I looked around for something else the next semester in place of drama classes and found a poetry workshop. Although I'd written poetry before, I had never taken it seriously, and didn't even really know what good poetry was. That first class, taught by the wonderful John Matthias, changed my life's path. John continues to be a mentor to me, in fact, and I have learned not just from his teachings but from his very magical and accomplished poems. I'm also grateful to Sonia

Gernes and Stephen Fredman, who provided guidance and helped me understand that poetry is my bliss.

KEVIN HART

While at the University of Notre Dame (2002–2007) I wrote all of *Young Rain* and some of *Morning Knowledge*. For the first time, I started translating from the Chinese (with the immense help of Gloria Davies), and I learned, and still learn, a great deal from conversations about poetry and poetics with Professor Henry Weinfield in the Program of Liberal Studies.

MARY KATHLEEN HAWLEY

Although I did not write poetry in a serious way until some years after college, the seeds of my future work were sown during my years at Notre Dame. As a sophomore, I took a poetry workshop with Sonia Gernes, and while my poems were forgettable, the habit of working with words was not. Then, in my junior year, I participated in LAPEL (the Latin American Program for Experiential Learning), living and working in a sprawling desert neighborhood of Lima, Peru. Along with two other Notre Dame students, I spent the year doing volunteer work and independent studies, overseen by Holy Cross priests Robert Plasker and Phil Devlin. As part of our course of study, they introduced us to the poetry of César Vallejo. It was Vallejo's poetry that helped me come to terms with the many paradoxes of that bleak landscape of sand dunes and shanty houses, a place of great poverty but also of hope. Vallejo expressed the despair of a world gone insane, and he wrestled with God as Jacob wrestled with the angel. I found comfort in the anger that drove some of his poems, and in the tenderness that permeated others, and I came to depend on his words. Though I didn't write much poetry for another eight years, for me that was the beginning of my life as a poet.

ORLANDO RICARDO MENES

I will just say briefly that during these last eight years teaching at Notre Dame, my poetry has matured and shifted in a new direction that is quite surprising to me still. I am now completing a volume consisting of poems in traditional stanzas, in particular the sonnet. I take delight in the tension that is created as I both submit to and resist this form.

JOYELLE McSWEENEY

The positive classroom experiences I've had at Notre Dame in my years here have benefited my writing immensely. The collaborative experiences of reading together, of watching texts unfold into still more texts, of teasing productive problems out of both published works and works-in-progress, all continually renew my interest in and love for literature and languages and spur on the permutations and exfoliations that make my work and brain buzz. I love the total immersion in letters and words and sentences and sounds and voices and gestures and unexpected euphonies and bountiful contaminations and aftereffects.

THOMAS O'GRADY

"Every poem should be made up of lines that are poems." So wrote Ralph Waldo Emerson in his "Journals," which I read in a graduate seminar on American Transcendentalism during my days as a doctoral student in English at Notre Dame in the early 1980s. I wonder now whether Emerson's assertion directly influenced the first line of poetry that I recall writing in the shadow of the Golden Dome: "The horse that ploughed back sod now plods backroads."

Or does that line, with its opening pair of high-stepping iambs giving way to a trio of heavy-hoofed spondees—all yoked together by alliteration, assonance, and consonance—owe a debt to Alexander Pope's musing on prosody in "An Essay on Criticism"? I read that treatise-in-verse for my Ph.D. comprehensive exams a year or two later: "When Ajax strives, some rock's vast weight to throw, / The line too labors, and the words move slow."

Eventually, that line with the trudging gait got harnessed into "A Fiddler's Share," a poem in which I equate my commitment to the poet's craft with my maternal great-uncle's dedication to playing his fiddle . . . which resulted in the loss of the family farm on Prince Edward Island: risky business!

So my writing about PEI—about my exile's relationship to that place of my birth, my boyhood, my youth—found its first wobbly legs during my five years at Notre Dame. From deep in the American heartland, I began to make my long poetic way back home.

JOHN PHILLIP SANTOS

I often say I went to *el otro* Notre Dame, an alternate universe Notre Dame of poets and artists, actors and philosophers, outliers to the ordinary world—Notre Dame's fellaheen, to coin a favorite Kerouacian Beat moniker. *El otro* Notre Dame was a crossroads of poets, which in my years included meeting and spending time with Jorge Luis Borges, Allen Ginsberg, Denise Levertov, William Stafford, Okot p'Bitek, Jackson Mac Low, and Robert Hass, to name just a few. It was an intimate community of scholar poets who shared work and fiesta. Whether in classes, or students among themselves, or at gatherings in the great poet-houses of Ernest Sandeen and John Matthias, at el *otro* Notre Dame, poetry was a serious, sometimes riotous business. Aesthetic quarrels flared up like prairie fires. Hardcore Poundians denounced Eliot imitators or denounced wet Poundians. I found the stirrings of a voice somewhere between Ernie's plain-spoken, compassionate mysterium of the everyday and John's discursive historico-literary-biographical hermeneutics. In *The Juggler*, some of us wrote neo-rustic Chicano Americana, some were searingly confessional, others used jagged hieroglyphic abstractions—an amazing array of voices. Above all, there was the sense that writing poetry mattered, a fragile, fleeting, radical hope that the world might be changed through poetic invention. For one coming from the Texas borderlands, a place beyond the reach of orthodox American literary tradition, my time at *el otro* Notre Dame connected me to some of the most powerful currents of that history and charged me to make my own way with it.

MICHAEL SMITH

It goes without saying that the most precious strength of a writing program is the time and freedom it provides its students. Anything else you get is gravy. Notre Dame provided me with the time and the freedom to work in luxurious quantities, but its faculty gave me, also, important models of how to be a working writer. Without parochial attachment to ideology, without self-protective insecurities, my teachers showed me what it meant to be catholic in my aesthetics and confident in my convictions.

ANTHONY WALTON

I can say, quite simply, that I would not have written poetry, which has loomed very large in my adult life, had I not attended Notre Dame. I had attempted to write songs and a few short stories while in high school; I continued dabbling in songwriting, and experimented with some very bad poems, which I showed to John Santos, the leading student writer at that time, who very generously read my "work." He (gently) pointed out some deficits along with strong points, and suggested that I get in touch with and try to work with John Matthias. This was not the first time that had been suggested; as I have written in detail elsewhere, Donald Sniegowski had previously pointed me in that direction; to my lasting good fortune, I went.

These memories are a roundabout way of answering the question that has been posed; when I think back about my time at the university, I think about the communities of artists and their willingness to be simultaneously welcoming and rigorous. When I got to Matthias's classes, I was both encouraged and challenged— challenged to meet the highest standards that Matthias and subsequently Ernest Sandeen and Douglas Kinsey (for, yes, I was also interested in visual arts) and a host of other professors held for themselves. The only option was to meet the standard or get out, and I have come to see such expectation as the greatest gift one can offer a young person, and as an example I have attempted to follow in my own career as a professor. I was taken seriously, and therefore challenged to take myself seriously—the only chance a young artist has to develop, much less succeed.

HENRY MICHAEL WEINFIELD

I am originally from Montreal, Canada, but before coming to Notre Dame in 1991, I lived in New York City for twenty-five years. I am essentially a "hellenized" Jew, so I consider it a minor miracle that I was offered a position in the Program of Liberal Studies, Notre Dame's Catholic great books department. Oddly enough, the shoe fit very well, and I consider myself exceedingly fortunate to have landed at Notre Dame. I have great love for PLS and for the university and have benefited in many ways from these affiliations, including from the standpoint of my poetry. In the PLS great book seminars, we are asked to teach many texts and in many different fields and areas outside our specialties, and some of the works I would never otherwise have taught have made an indelible impression on me. Probably most important for me has been Dante's *Divine Comedy*. I have a poem entitled "August: The Lake at Notre Dame," which is included in my new volume, *Without Mythologies: New and Selected Poems and Translations* (Dos Madres Press, 2008), which has an epigraph from Dante, and which I obviously would never have written had I not come to the university. In addition, I have written quite a few occasional poems, sometimes to be recited at PLS gatherings, that have emerged from texts or situations related to my teaching. Obviously, my poetry comes out of my life, and my life has been lived very substantially at Notre Dame, so it's impossible that I would not have been influenced by my time there. The translation of Hesiod's *Theogony* and *Works and Days*, which the University of Michigan Press published in 2006, would never have been accomplished—or even dreamed of—if not for Notre Dame. It was Catherine Schlegel of the Notre Dame Classics Department who introduced me to Hesiod in a serious way, and this led to the collaboration that produced our verse translation. One last thought: I often joke that I had to come to Notre Dame to get in touch with my Jewish roots. So, who knows: maybe even my "Hebrew Melodies" (a sequence of poems included in *Without Mythologies)* were influenced by the years I have spent at Our Lady's University.

JOHN WILKINSON

Arriving at Notre Dame, I felt like an ethnographer. A secular Englishman, I had thought that a year in Manhattan and some traveling on the West Coast meant that I was familiar with the United States. Now, not only had I left England for a Catholic university in the Midwest, but in my middle age I was reinventing myself as an academic, and as a professional—that is, salaried—poet. All this would have been unimaginable to me a few years before. Subsequently, I have become to some extent my own ethnographer, separating from an earlier self while not quite absorbed by the new world I inhabit.

What can I disentangle here which I might attribute specifically to Notre Dame? Most important is what this anthology represents. I have been astonished to find Notre Dame the centre of such ambitious poetical activity; both in the poetry written, and in its academic programme of poetics. Nor is this happenstance. Oddly, much as Irish monks once preserved an imperiled classical learning, so this Catholic and Irish and American place takes more seriously the safekeeping of a secular European tradition of the humanities than do Europe's great universities. Here such a tradition encounters African American and Latino traditions, among others, and continues its centuries-old productive quarrel with religion. I find it a good place to be, whoever I am.

Biographies of the Poets

Francisco Aragón is the author of *Puerta del Sol* (Bilingual Press) and editor of the award-winning *The Wind Shifts: New Latino Poetry* (University of Arizona Press). His work has appeared in a range of anthologies, including *Inventions of Farewell: A Book of Elegies* (W. W. Norton), *American Diaspora: Poetry of Displacement* (University of Iowa Press), and, more recently, *Evensong: Contemporary American Poets on Spirituality* (Bottom Dog Press) and *Deep Travel: Contemporary American Poets Abroad* (Ninebark Press). He directs Letras Latinas, the literary program of the Institute for Latino Studies (ILS) at Notre Dame. He is also the editor of Canto Cosas, a new book series from Bilingual Press featuring new Latino and Latina poets. A native of San Francisco, he resides in Arlington, Virginia, and works out of the ILS office in Washington, D.C. He received his M.F.A. from Notre Dame in 2003.

Robert Archambeau (M.F.A.; Ph.D. 1996) was born in the United States but lived in Canada for most of his life, before returning for graduate study at the University of Notre Dame. He has taught at Lund University in Sweden and at Lake Forest College, where he is currently on the faculty. Formerly the editor of the poetry review *Samizdat*, he now co-directs the &NOW Festival of Innovative Writing. His books include *Word Play Place: Essays on the Poetry of John Matthias*, *Home and Variations* (a collection of poems), and *Laureates and Heretics: Six Careers in American Poetry*.

Bei Dao (Zhao Zhenkai) was born in Beijing in 1949 and is generally regarded as one of the foremost Chinese poets writing today.

261

Karni Pal Bhati teaches at Furman University in South Carolina and is the author of *On Another Ground* (Ninety-Six Press, 2006).

Kimberly M. Blaeser is a professor at the University of Wisconsin, Milwaukee, where she teaches Creative Writing and Native American Literature. She earned her M.A. and Ph.D. from the University of Notre Dame. Her publications include three books of poetry: *Trailing You*, winner of the first book award from the Native Writers' Circle of the Americas, *Absentee Indians and Other Poems*, and *Apprenticed to Justice*. Her scholarly study *Gerald Vizenor: Writing in the Oral Tradition* was the first native-authored book-length study of an indigenous author. Of Anishinaabe ancestry and an enrolled member of the Minnesota Chippewa, Blaeser, who grew up on the White Earth Reservation, is also the editor of *Stories Migrating Home: A Collection of Anishinaabe Prose* and *Traces in Blood, Bone, and Stone: Contemporary Ojibwe Poetry*. Her recent scholarly publications include a hundred-page essay on Native poetry, "Cannons and Canonization," in *The Columbia Guide to American Indian Literatures of the United States*.

Jenny Boully is the author of *The Book of Beginnings and Endings* (Sarabande), *[one love affair]** (Tarpaulin Sky Press), and *The Body: An Essay* (Essay Press). Her chapbook, *Moveable Types*, is available from Noemi Press. Her work has been anthologized in *The Next American Essay* (Graywolf), *Best American Poetry 2002* (Scribner), *Great American Prose Poems* (Scribner), and *Language for a New Century* (W. W. Norton). Born in Thailand and reared in Texas, she has studied at Hollins University and the University of Notre Dame (M.F.A. 2002). She is a Ph.D. Candidate at the Graduate Center of the City University of New York and currently teaches creative writing at Columbia College in Chicago.

Jacque Vaught Brogan is the author of *Damage* (University of Notre Dame Press, 2003) and a book-length experimental poem called *ta(l)king eyes* (CHAX Press, 2009), as well as over fifty other poems published in journals that range from *The Formalist* to the feminist, experimentalist journal *How(ever)*. She has been the featured essayist and poet for *Poetry International* and the featured poet for *Spring: The*

E. E. Cummings Journal and *Connotations*. She is a professor in the English Department at Notre Dame and the author of several critical books and articles on poetry.

Stacy Cartledge is the author of a book of poems, *Within the Space Between* (Spuyten Duyvil Press). His chapbook, *Topography*, was published by Wild Honey Press. He is currently the poetry editor of *The Georgetown Review* and teaches poetry and writing courses at Georgetown College.

Michael Coffey (B.A. 1976) has published three books of poems and a book on baseball (*27 Men Out: Baseball's Perfect Games*). He was co-editor of *The Irish in America*, a companion volume to a three-part PBS documentary on Irish immigration. He is currently executive managing editor at *Publishers Weekly*.

Seamus Deane is emeritus professor of English and Donald and Marilyn Keough Professor of Irish Studies at the University of Notre Dame. He is a member of the Royal Irish Academy, a founding director of the Field Day Theatre Company, the general editor of Joyce in the Penguin Classic Series, and the author of several books, including *A Short History of Irish Literature*; *Celtic Revivals*; *Essays in Modern Irish Literature*; *The French Revolution and Enlightenment in England*; and *Strange Country: Modernity and the Nation*.

Joe Francis Doerr lives in Austin, Texas, with his wife Mary. He is the author of *Order of the Ordinary* (Salt Publishing) and teaches writing at St. Edward's University.

Kevin Ducey was born in Ohio and studied English, film, and history at the University of Colorado, Boulder, before his two years at Notre Dame (M.F.A. 2003–2004). He was the winner of the prestigious APR/Honickman First Book Prize in 2004 for his collection *Rhinoceros*.

Cornelius Eady, born in Rochester, New York, is the author of eight books of poetry, most recently *Hardheaded Weather* (2008). He has received the Prairie Schooner Strousse Award and fellowships from the

National Endowment for the Arts, the John Simon Guggenheim Foundation, the Lila Wallace–Reader's Digest Foundation, and the Rockefeller Foundation. In 1996, Eady and poet Toi Derricote founded Cave Canem, a non-profit organization for black poets. He was associate professor of English at Notre Dame from 2005 until 2010.

Beth Ann Fennelly (B.A. 1993) received a 2003 National Endowment for the Arts Award and a 2006 United States Artist grant. She has written three books of poetry, *Open House,* which won The 2001 *Kenyon Review* Prize and the GLCA New Writers Award; *Tender Hooks* (W. W. Norton, 2004); and *Unmentionables* (W. W. Norton, 2008). She has been included three times in the *Best American Poetry* series and is a Pushcart Prize winner. She is an associate professor at the University of Mississippi.

Kevin Hart's most recent poetry collections are *Flame Tree: Selected Poems* (Bloodaxe Books, 2002), *Young Rain* (Bloodaxe Books/University of Notre Dame Press, 2008), and *Morning Knowledge* (University of Notre Dame Press, 2011). Among his scholarly books, he is the coeditor of *The Exorbitant: Emmanuel Levinas between Jews and Christians* (Fordham University Press, 2010) and editor of *Clandestine Encounters: Philosophy in the Narratives of Maurice Blanchot* (University of Notre Dame Press, 2010). He is Edwin B. Kyle Professor of Christian Studies at the University of Virginia, where he also holds professorships in the Department of English and the Department of French.

Mary Kathleen Hawley (B.A. 1979) is the author of *Double Tongues* and co-translator of a bilingual poetry anthology, *Astillas de luz/Shards of Light,* both published by Tía Chucha Press. She has been active in the Chicago poetry community for many years, and her poems have appeared in various journals and anthologies, including *Notre Dame Review, The Bloomsbury Review, Luna, Another Chicago Magazine,* and *Power Lines: A Decade of Poetry from Chicago's Guild Complex.*

Joyelle McSweeney is the author of two books of poetry: *The Red Bird* (Fence Books, 2002), which was selected for the first Fence Modern

Poets Series Prize by Allen Grossman; and *The Commandrine and Other Poems* (Fence Books, 2004). In 2007 she published two lyric novels: *Nylund, the Sarcographer*, a baroque *noir* from Tarpaulin Sky Press, and *Flet*, a science fiction from Fence Books. With Johannes Göransson, she is the co-founder of Action Books and *Action, Yes*, a press and Web quarterly, respectively, for international writing and hybrid forms. She is currently at work on a multigenre translation of the *Aeneid*.

Orlando Ricardo Menes is associate professor in the Creative Writing Program at the University of Notre Dame. His poems have appeared in several anthologies, as well as literary magazines, including *Ploughshares*, *The Antioch Review*, *Shenandoah*, *Prairie Schooner*, *Chelsea*, *Callaloo*, *Indiana Review*, *North American Review*, *New Letters*, *Third Coast*, and *Green Mountains Review*. His collection *Furia* was published in 2005 by Milkweed Editions. He is also the author of *Rumba atop the Stones* (Peepal Tree Press, 2001), as well as editor of the anthology *Renaming Ecstasy: Latino Writings on the Sacred* (Bilingual Press/Editorial Bilingüe, 2004).

Thomas O'Grady was born and grew up on Prince Edward Island. He was educated at the University of PEI, University College Dublin, and the University of Notre Dame (1979–1984). He is currently professor of English, Director of Irish Studies, and a member of the Creative Writing faculty at the University of Massachusetts, Boston. He lives in Milton, Massachusetts, with his wife and three daughters. His first book of poems, *What Really Matters*, was published in the Hugh MacLennan Poetry Series in April 2000 by McGill-Queen's University Press (and reprinted in September 2000). He has completed the manuscript for a second volume of poems, *Makeover*, as well as a manuscript for a volume of short fiction, *The Great Antonio and Other Stories*.

John Phillip Santos (B.A. 1979) is an author and documentary producer living in San Antonio, Texas. His first book *Places Unfinished at the Time of Creation* was a finalist for the National Book Award in 1999. A sequel, *The Farthest Home Is in an Empire of Fire*, was published by Viking/Penguin in 2010. Poems in this volume are from *Songs Older than Any Known Singer* (Wings, 2007).

Michael Smith (M.F.A. 2001) is the author of *How to Make a Mummy* (CustomWords, 2008). His poems have appeared, or are forthcoming, in *Carolina Quarterly, Hotel Amerika, Quarter after Eight, Nebraska Review, Notre Dame Review, North American Review,* and *Iowa Review.* He currently teaches at Delta State University in Mississippi and was Writer-in-Residence in the Literature Department at American University in 2006–2007.

Anthony Walton is the author of *Mississippi: An American Journey,* a *New York Times* Notable Book for 1996; and a chapbook of poems, *Cricket Weather* (Blackberry Press). His poems have appeared in *The New Yorker, Notre Dame Review,* and *Kenyon Review,* among many other journals and magazines. His prose and journalism have been published in *The New York Times, Harper's, Atlantic Monthly,* and *The Oxford American.* He is also the editor, with Michael S. Harper, of the poetry anthologies *Every Shut-Eye Ain't Asleep,* and *The Vintage Book of African American Poetry.* A 1982 graduate of Notre Dame, he is currently Writer-in-Residence at Bowdoin College in Brunswick, Maine.

Henry Weinfield is a poet, translator, and literary scholar, and a professor in the Program of Liberal Studies at the University of Notre Dame. He is the author of several collections of poetry, including *The Sorrows of Eros and Other Poems* (University of Notre Dame Press, 1999); a translation of and commentary on the *Collected Poems of Stephane Mallarmé* (University of California Press, 1995); and a literary study, *The Poet Without a Name: Gray's Elegy and the Problem of History* (Southern Illinois University Press, 1991). His verse translation of Hesiod's *Works and Days* and *Theogony* (with Catherine Schlegel of the Classics Department) was published by the University of Michigan Press in 2006. He is working on a book on the blank verse tradition in English poetry, and recently completed a book on the American poets George Oppen and William Bronk.

John Wilkinson joined the University of Notre Dame in January 2005, first as Writer-in-Residence at the Keough-Naughton Institute for Irish Studies, and more recently as Research Professor in the Department of English. His books of poetry are published by Salt, most recently *Lake Shore Drive* (2006). In 2007, Salt published his collection of essays, *The Lyric Touch: Essays on the Poetry of Excess*. Before arriving at Notre Dame he worked in London as a performance manager and strategic planner in the British National Health Service.